P9-DEV-672

·TEN·
DINNER
PARTIES
-FOR TWO-

FRANCES BISSELL

·TEN·
DINNER
PARTIES
—FOR TWO—

INTERLINK BOOKS
An Imprint of Interlink Publishing Group, Inc.
NEW YORK

First American edition published 1989 by
INTERLINK BOOKS
An imprint of Interlink Publishing Group, Inc.
99 Seventh Avenue
Brooklyn, New York 11215

Originally published in Great Britain by Ebury Press 1988

Copyright © 1988 Sheldrake Publishing Ltd

Main text copyright © 1988 Frances Bissell

Designed and produced by
Sheldrake Press Ltd
188 Cavendish Road
London SW12 0DA

Library of Congress Cataloging-in-Publication Data

Bissell, Frances.
   Ten dinner parties for two / Frances Bissell. — 1st American ed.
      p.   cm.
   Includes index.
   ISBN 0-940793-30-X : $19.95
      1. Dinners and dining.   2. Cookery for two.   3. Menus.   I. Title.
II. Title.   10 dinner parties for 2.
TX737.854   1989
641.5'61—dc20   89-32090
                                                                          CIP

ISBN 0-940793-30-X

All rights reserved under International and Pan-American Copyright
Conventions. No part of this book may be reproduced or utilized in
any form or by any means, electronic or mechanical, including
photocopying, recording, or by information storage and retrieval
systems, without permission in writing from the publisher.

EDITOR: SIMON RIGGE
Managing Editor: Eleanor Lines
Deputy Managing Editor: Nina Shandloff
Art Direction and Book Design: Ivor Claydon, Bob Hook
Photography: Graham Miller assisted by Nicholas Rigg
Home Economist: Maxine Clark
Stylist: Pip Kelly
Artwork: Christopher White
Assistant Editors: Joanna Edwards, Diana Vowles
Sub-Editor: Norma MacMillan
Production Manager: Hugh Allan
Production Assistants: Rebecca Bone, Helen Seccombe
Editorial Assistant: Helen Ridge

Printed in Hong Kong by Imago Publishing

THE AUTHOR
Frances Bissell's weekly columns in *The Times* of London have brought
her a large following among the aficionados of the art of food writing.
She also contributes regularly to a number of magazines, among them
Homes and Gardens, Harpers and Queen and *Harpers Bazaar*, as well as
being featured in *The New York Times* and *San Francisco Examiner*. Her
two previous books are *A Cook's Calendar* and *The Pleasures of Cookery*.

FOR TOM

CONTENTS

Introduction

Cooking food according to its season has always been very important to me, both for practical reasons as well as more intangible ones. Food cooked and eaten during its growing and harvesting season reaches us in a much fresher condition and is better in texture, smell and flavor than if it has been stored. You have only to think of the delightful aroma of the first English apples as they appear in August and September to know what I mean. Although it is unlikely to be so, they actually smell as if they had been picked a moment ago. Summer and early autumn tomatoes sometimes still have that freshly picked "green" smell by the time they reach the stores.

I love the feasting that comes with an abundance of fruit and vegetables and would positively enjoy eating fresh tomatoes every day for weeks and weeks given the chance. Those of us who live in an urban society are quite removed from this aspect of the seasons. This summer my father wrote to me about tomatoes. My parents live on a small, quiet Mediterranean island, Gozo, where gardening is one of their main pursuits; it has taken them some while to get used to the difference in the seasons. From carefully nurturing a few tomato plants in a greenhouse in an exposed corner of Derbyshire, right up in England's Peak District, they were faced here with tomatoes ripening non-stop from July to September. Outdoors! And farmer friends would give them greenhouse tomatoes from April onwards, by the bushel. Hot tomato soups, chilled tomato soups, tomato purée for the freezer, tomato sauces for fish, tomatoes broiled for breakfast and toasted with cheese for lunch, chutneys made from green and from ripe tomatoes, and bottles and bottles of deliciously rich tomato juice: my parents prepared tomatoes in all these ways and more, and begged me for yet more recipes. When my husband, Tom, and I visited them at the end of the summer, tomatoes were still to be found, and we dried them on the roof to make them into that extraordinarily expensive delicacy, sun-dried tomatoes, which is to be found in exclusive specialty stores. We brought bags of them back, which I then packed into jars filled with olive oil. Winter pasta dishes benefited from that hint of Mediterranean summer, but it was nothing like the real thing, nothing like munching fresh warm tomatoes crushed with sea salt and garlic onto bread trickled with olive oil taken straight from a wood-fired oven. And as for the tomatoes to be found in our stores during the winter . . . well, we will not speak of these here, and you will not find any need for fresh tomatoes in any of the winter dinner menus.

Just as my parents have had to readjust their thinking about the seasons so have I, living, shopping and cooking in north London where, it seems, every imaginable ingredient is available, at all times of the year. It seems, too, that those who export foodstuffs to Britain often choose their produce much more carefully than our growers and suppliers at home. I have seen asparagus from Australia often looking greener and fresher than asparagus from Suffolk. This makes it very hard to resist buying food out of season. I begin to ask myself, "Why should I wait for the English asparagus season in spring if I can buy beautiful green, fresh, crisp asparagus from Australia in November?" Especially when it costs no more per pound than, say, sirloin steak? I know which I would prefer to make a meal out of.

Often, then, the notion of a seasonal menu or ingredient is no more than an atavistic memory of our forebears' eating patterns. But Nature is clever. Just when she's let us think we have her beaten, she reminds us that you can, indeed, only get green English walnuts in November, and glasswort in the summer. These truly seasonal treats have an honored place in the meals I cook at home, served by themselves as simply and as naturally as possible. There is an inexplicable feeling of "rightness" about preparing and eating something in season. One is brought closer to the natural rhythm of events and one is reminded that cooking and eating are very basic human activities, despite all the fads and fashions that attach to them.

For me, cooking is also a means of giving. I am not rich enough to buy for those I love the sort of gifts I would like to give them, and that I think they deserve, but I can cook for them and feed them. With them I share the pleasure I take in cooking, with them I share delicious food. I take delight in creating a meal especially for them, one they have never eaten before and one I have never cooked for anyone else. My shopping for such meals is usually only sketchily planned, which allows me to pounce on the unexpected delicacy or just-now-remembered ingredient that will surely appeal to the . . . what? The eater? The recipient? The diner? The sharer? The guest, I think.

Even though Tom and I have been sharing meals for many years, he waits to be invited to the table when dinner is ready. Occasionally he cooks dinner, and I am then the guest. It is our favorite part of the day, not just because we love food and wine, but because that period at the table is a time for quiet, for conversation, for plans, for sharing the things that concern us. The food nourishes our bodies and prepares us for the next day, but our minds and spirits are also nourished and strengthened by the other things we have shared.

Writing this book has been sheer self-indulgence. I have been given license to write about what I like doing best. The recipes are designed to be sufficient for two people; the only exceptions are where the basic ingredients, method or cooking equipment dictate larger quantities. Occasionally, anticipating the availability of leftovers, I have recommended buying more ingredients than are strictly necessary to prepare a particular recipe. For example, when making the Oxtail Stew (page 88) I suggest buying enough oxtail to make an Oxtail Terrine as well (page 86): the terrine will provide for extra guests at a lunch party, and is very well worth doing. In our house hold, every day we are at home brings a dinner party at the end of it, a dinner party for two. It might not be a five-course meal – simply a salad, some good pasta with a homemade sauce and some cheese and fruit. But there will be a tablecloth, linen napkins, appropriate wine, flowers, a candle in winter, an open window in summer, and time to enjoy the food, the conversation and each other's company. This book is for anyone and everyone to whom food is for sharing.

SOME NOTES ON MY PANTRY AND KITCHEN

For someone whose cooking is based very much on the availability of fresh produce and who does not rely on a freezer or microwave oven, it is surprising how well filled my pantry is.

What are all those cans and jars doing there? A closer look reveals that much shelf space is taken up with last year's harvest of jams and jellies, some for us and some for presents. More often than not they are the kind to serve with meat and game rather than to spread on bread. A few jars contain other preserves – dried tomatoes in olive oil, pickled lemons, capers, glasswort in a sweet and sour brine. All these have been collected on foraging trips, whether to Gozo, Sicily or Norfolk, wrapped and transported with care, and then preserved as appropriate to be dipped into in the future as a reminder of those travels.

In fact, my pantry can be likened to a photograph album. Most of the items in it recall a place we have been to or a visit we've received from friends. The small boxes of wild rice, the bag of blue corn with its distinctive picture on the front and the shiny pecans are all mementos of Barbara and Howard's visit from San Francisco. They always bring us news of the latest food fashions and, indeed, some of the latest fashionable food. Dried mushrooms and a red and gold tin of Ti Kuan Yin tea are souvenirs of one of our visits to Hong Kong. Looking at them reminds me of the morning I spent with chef Chan Fat Chee, first on a visit round his local market in Hong Kong's New Territories, then to the herbalist where he showed me how to choose the best dried mushrooms and finally back to his kitchen where he demonstrated how to cook them, stuffed with a delicate fresh shrimp paste.

My pantry also contains all the useful standbys. Cans of chickpeas, borlotti beans and flageolets are used in soups, salads and dips. Anchovies and sardines in olive oil for making into flavored butters and for quick snacks and salad ingredients are worth giving shelf space to. Cans of Italian plum tomatoes, from San Marzano if I can get them, are indispensable throughout the long months when sweet, ripe tomatoes are unavailable. I probably get through four cans a week for soups and casseroles. At least two cans go into the batch of homemade tomato sauce I like to make at the beginning of the week to serve with gnocchi or pasta when we want just a simple supper. Oils and vinegars I find quite irresistible. They are always on my shopping list wherever we travel and not just on our visits to Italy. Although extra virgin olive oil from Tuscany is, indeed, one of the finest products this earth has to offer, one does wonder where much of the Tuscan extra virgin oil now coming onto the market is really grown. A bad frost wiped out the olive groves some years ago. Olive trees take 50 years to reach their peak. Fortunately, we have catholic tastes, and our pantry is just as likely to house extra virgin olive oil from Tunisia and California as from Spain and Portugal. All are different in character. All are delicious.

Bottles of hazelnut, walnut, almond and sesame oil are all used regularly, in salads and in marinating fish particularly.

From a good basic white or red wine vinegar I now make my own flavored vinegars – garlic, tomato (using cherry tomatoes), pear, blueberry, blackberry and all the fragrant herb vinegars. I store them on the kitchen windowsill in old decanters and strangely shaped bottles through which the light filters gently.

Fads and fashions are also reflected in my pantry. Lurking behind the cans of tomatoes, trying to disguise themselves as jam, I see small jars of pink peppercorns. Do you remember them? Once upon a time, a *magret de canard* could not be seen in public without its obligatory decoration of strategically placed pink peppercorns. A rumour that they were injurious to health led to a fear that we soon would not be able to buy them, and so I stocked up. Clearly, many other people did the same, for I have noticed them slowly creeping back into fashion. Not long ago I was served, by one of the best chefs in London, a plate of salmon delicately marinated in a dressing containing a few pink peppercorns. During the same week I ate a marvelous game terrine studded with them. Perhaps it is just as well that I kept them in what Tom often refers to as "hoarder's corner." As I unpack some delectable dried morels or a special jar of honey, I hear Tom ask plaintively, "Do we get to eat that, or is it going into hoarder's corner?" I do, I am afraid, have a tendency to squirrel things away for a rainy day.

The contents of my pantry overflow onto my worktops. Jars of spaghetti, wheat kernels, rice, couscous and bulgur sit next to the coffee grinder and the tea kettle. The vegetable basket, actually the bottom half of a chicken brick, sits huddled up between the electric steamer and the food processor. And that is about the extent of my kitchen gadgetry. In a tiny, ill-planned kitchen such as mine everything has to earn its place. The blender/grinder and the steamer both do so. The food processor just qualifies – it is simple and a joy to use for the right job, but it's such a bother to wash and store away.

What about the refrigerator? Well, we need it for the white wine and champagne. And milk and fruit juice. Little else goes into it apart from salad greens for a couple of days and perhaps a piece of meat marinating or salmon turning into gravadlax. There will be a pot or two of yogurt, the thick, strained Greek or Lebanese type that is delicious to eat either by itself or with honey for a quick dessert or to use in cooking. As you will see from the recipes that follow, I often use it in place of cream. On the other hand, I will sometimes treat myself to a large pot of *crème fraîche* if we are in France – it, too, is wonderful for cooking. The tiny freezer compartment is used for ice, spinach (the only frozen vegetable I use), pita bread (to keep it fresh longer) and small packs of filo pastry. Nothing else. It is not the sort of refrigerator you can open in the hope of finding something to munch on, but there will almost certainly be a large bowl of stock from which I can make a soup.

Overleaf are my four basic stock recipes. They will be useful for the sauces and soups in the menus I have suggested, but also for your own inventions. The recipes that I have put together for different occasions with particular wines are combinations we have enjoyed, but the menus are not intended to be prescriptive; they are there to give you ideas with which to experiment.

BASIC RECIPES

VEGETABLE STOCK

INGREDIENTS

2/3 cup orange lentils or split peas

2 onions, sliced

2 carrots, sliced

2 celery stalks, sliced

1 leek, sliced (optional)

1 bunch watercress

several sprigs of parsley

2 bay leaves

sprig of thyme or rosemary

3 in curl of orange or lemon zest

12 black or mixed peppercorns

6 juniper berries

6 allspice berries

a few mushrooms (optional)

approx 5 pints water

Makes approx 1 quart stock

This is the stock I like to use for vegetable soup. If you are cooking for vegetarians it is also the ideal base for sauces as it has plenty of flavor, particularly when reduced and concentrated. For a richer color, add one or two pieces of the onion skin to the stock (not the coarse outer skin but the inner golden one). Alternatively, you could fry some of the onion first to caramelize it before adding it to the stock. Liquid caramel is often used as a food coloring and it is a simple matter to produce this effect yourself by browning some onion or, indeed, carrots or other vegetables. The browning is the sugar in the vegetable being burnt by the heat of the frying pan.

Wash and drain the lentils or split peas and put all the ingredients in a large saucepan. Bring to a boil, skim any foam off its surface, cover partially and simmer for 1 to 1½ hours. Strain the stock through a scalded, cheesecloth-lined sieve, return it to a clean saucepan and boil to reduce to 1 quart. Cool rapidly and refrigerate unless you are using the stock at once. Do not keep for more than 48 hours in the refrigerator.

LIGHT MEAT STOCK

INGREDIENTS

3 lb veal bones

1 or 2 pig's feet, chopped in half

6–8 chicken wings or 1 lb chicken pieces

1 onion, roughly chopped

2 celery stalks, roughly chopped

2 carrots, roughly chopped

1 leek, roughly chopped (optional)

12 black or mixed peppercorns

2 bay leaves

a few parsley stems

3 in curl of orange or lemon zest

3½ quarts water

Makes approx 5 cups stock

The addition of the pig's feet gives a marvelously rich jelly when the stock has cooled and set. When the pig's feet are completely cooked, but before they disintegrate, I carefully remove them from the stock pot, allow them to cool enough to handle them, then roll them in melted butter and soft white bread crumbs and bake them in the oven or under the broiler to make an inexpensive and delicious meal. Serve with a watercress salad and a mustardy mayonnaise.

This stock can be used as a base for soup or sauce. Do not salt it since, particularly in the latter case, the stock will often need to be reduced and thus concentrated. Salting to taste at the stock stage would produce far too salty a sauce.

Trim any fat from the veal bones and put them in a large saucepan with the rest of the ingredients. Bring to a boil, remove any scum that forms on the surface, lower the heat and simmer gently, partially covered, for 3 to 4 hours. You can leave the stock pot on a very low heat overnight, but you must be sure that it does simmer – that is, it must reach boiling point from time to time. If it is on too low a heat it could become an unhealthy breeding ground for bacteria.

Strain the stock through a sieve lined with scalded cheesecloth. Return it to a clean saucepan and reduce it to 5 cups. Cool it as rapidly as possible, then refrigerate. Do not keep for more than 3 to 4 days.

FISH STOCK

INGREDIENTS

1 tsp olive oil or sunflower oil
1 onion, chopped or sliced
1 carrot, chopped
1 celery stalk, chopped
1 leek, chopped
watercress, parsley, fennel, etc. – whatever is available
1–2 squashy tomatoes
1¾ lb fish bones and pieces, chopped to fit your saucepan
1 quart water

Makes approx 1 quart

Since a number of the recipes call for fish stock, here is my standard and very adaptable recipe as a base for sauces or soups. If, for example, you are buying sole, ask your fish man to fillet it and wrap the bones, head and skin separately, together with any other bones he or she can spare. I do not like the flavor given by shrimp shells and trimmings and would not normally use them, but lobster shells are another matter.

Whenever possible, try to make your stock well in advance and with plenty of ventilation. Regrettably the smell of fish stock does linger in the kitchen, and also in your hair and in your clothes.

Rub the olive or sunflower oil around a heavy saucepan and turn the vegetables in the pan until *just* beginning to turn color. Add the fish bones and pieces and cook until opaque. Pour on the water and bring slowly to a boil. Simmer gently, covered, for 40 minutes. Strain. Cool and refrigerate until required. Do not season at this stage since the stock will often need to be much reduced for a sauce and salting it now will ruin the end result.

CHICKEN STOCK

INGREDIENTS

8 chicken wings
1 medium onion, sliced
1 carrot, sliced
1 celery stalk, sliced
1 leek, sliced
watercress and parsley stems (2 or 3 of each)
12 black peppercorns
5 pints water

Makes approx 2½ pints stock

Herbs such as chervil and tarragon can also be used for flavoring this stock. Pungent ones such as rosemary or sage are not recommended – they would overwhelm the chicken flavor.

A cooked chicken carcass can also be used to produce a chicken stock, using exactly the same method, but do not expect to get the same depth of flavor.

Put all the ingredients in a large saucepan. Bring to a boil and skim any foam off the surface. Lower the heat, partially cover and simmer for 2 hours. Strain the stock through a sieve lined with scalded cheesecloth. Return it to a clean saucepan and reduce it to 2½ pints. Cool it as rapidly as possible, then refrigerate. Do not keep for more than 3 days.

Spring

FLAVORS

The pale yellows, green and white of the food give this meal a sense of spring that would look good carried through into the table's appearance. Think about flowers that pick up the fresh yellows and cool greens. You could use sunny yellows in November or January – it is just the time of year when you begin to see mimosa. How that would brighten up the winter gloom! As well as Australian asparagus, I have also found new potatoes – English Maris Pipers – in November, while quail eggs are available all year round – so I can recreate a meal of spring flavors at almost any time.

I have already adapted the idea of potatoes as a shell for other ingredients to a number of recipes and, as well as the recipe with quail eggs, I have given one with snails. Try also shrimp or chopped mushrooms; the latter are particularly good with potatoes. I have also liked a version with tiny cubes of goat cheese with chives or chopped scallions. These recipes, like most of the others throughout the book, are enormously adaptable according, not just to my tastes, but to yours, and to your imagination. It would make me very happy if I were to hear one day that someone had bought this book and not used a single recipe in it but had gone on to devise new recipes based on mine.

For one of our very favorite meals I steam or boil asparagus and new potatoes, as many as we can eat, and serve them with fried, poached or boiled eggs, the egg yolk serving as a dip for the asparagus tips, the potatoes then eaten with the asparagus stalks.

At this time of year our grandmothers and great grandmothers thought it was a good idea to give the system a spring-cleaning after a long winter of rich food. Dandelions were thought to be appropriate, and I have used these in a Hedgerow Salad.

Italy was the source of inspiration for my risotto recipe. I have never actually tasted asparagus risotto there, but the

Quail Eggs Baked in New Potatoes
or
Snails Baked in New Potatoes

Asparagus and White Wine Risotto

Cod Fillets with Beet Sauce
Hedgerow Salad
with Walnut and Arugula Dressing

Light Lemon and Hazelnut Sponge
Cake

principle of good stock, the right kind of rice and a small quantity of prime flavoring ingredients applies. From this recipe you can develop, as I have done, countless risottos. My favorites are those using vegetables. Sometimes I use new season vegetables when they are still expensive, as this is a means of making a little go a long way. I might take a fairly ordinary vegetable and turn it into a special dish; finely chopped celery and carrot is one combination I like. I have also made it with pumpkin, with zucchini and with radicchio. Sadly, the latter does not keep its rich garnet color as it browns in cooking but the distinctive bitter flavor remains, which is why I use it.

The Cod Fillets with Beet Sauce sit as a wonderful contrast to the pale, delicate dishes before and after. I have included them for their vivid, delicious sauce, to remind people that it is possible to serve really quite a wide range of vegetables and flavorings with fish. The beet sauce works well with any fish and, of course, the dish is not a seasonal one – although cod is certainly at its best between October and April.

If you were to remove the cod recipe, and cook extra risotto, this would be an excellent meal for vegetarians. Use, in that case, vegetable stock or water in the risotto rather than chicken stock.

Fresh, light flavors are carried right through to the end of the meal in the form of a Lemon and Hazelnut Sponge Cake. The lively flavors of this menu suggest fresh, lively wines. Something gently sparkling would be entirely appropriate and would be clean enough to clear the palate after the eggs and the creamy risotto. Vinho Verde, the "green" wine of northern Portugal, would accompany all the savory dishes very well. It is a light wine, low in alcohol, and more and more of it is available as it is drunk in Portugal and not slightly sweetened for export. A more expensive wine, and more "serious" altogether, is Prosecco. This dry sparkling wine from the Veneto, around Conegliano and Valdobbiene, is delicious with food and a natural accompaniment to fish and vegetable dishes, being not astringently dry but full and rounded. Since it is not yet very widely exported (although the situation is, I am glad to say, better than it was a couple of years ago), Prosecco is one of the things we always look forward to on our visits to northern Italy. As well as being good with food, it also makes a most delightful apéritif.

TIMING

Quite a lot of preparation for this dinner can be done in advance but most of the dishes require quick, last–minute cooking. For meals of this sort, an extra seat for your guest and two apéritifs in the kitchen is quite a nice idea.

The cake can be baked and decorated several hours before dinner – say, in the morning. The potatoes can be par-boiled, cooled, then filled, covered and put to one side for an hour or so before cooking. The fish can be prepared and covered ready for baking, and the sauce made in advance. The risotto is definitely a dish to be cooked and prepared *à la minute*.

QUAIL EGGS BAKED IN NEW POTATOES

INGREDIENTS

6 small potatoes, weighing 2 oz each

salt and freshly ground pepper

2 tbsp unsalted butter, melted

6 quail eggs

Serves 2

Wash and scrub the potatoes. If new they should not need peeling. With the larger scoop of a melon baller, scoop out a hollow in each potato, and remove a very thin slice from the bottom to allow it to stand flat. Put the hollowed-out potatoes in a pan of salted water, bring to a boil and boil briskly until *just* cooked. Drain.

Preheat the oven to 350°.

Brush the potatoes inside and out with melted butter, season lightly and stand them on an oiled baking sheet. Carefully crack a quail egg into each potato. Place in the top half of the oven and bake for 8 to 10 minutes. Serve immediately, with a few salad leaves if you like.

SNAILS BAKED IN NEW POTATOES

INGREDIENTS

6 small potatoes, weighing 2 oz each

4 tbsp unsalted butter, softened

1 tbsp finely chopped fresh parsley

salt and freshly ground pepper

3 garlic cloves, crushed

6 canned snails

Serves 2

Prepare and par-boil the potatoes as in the previous recipe.

Make garlic butter by mixing together the butter, parsley, salt, pepper and garlic. Place a snail in each hollowed-out potato and fill up the hollow with garlic butter.

Preheat the oven to 350°.

Bake for 8 to 10 minutes, and serve with a little salad.

Opposite: Quail Eggs Baked in New Potatoes

ASPARAGUS AND WHITE WINE RISOTTO

INGREDIENTS

4 tbsp unsalted butter

1 small onion, sliced

1¼ cups Chicken or Vegetable Stock

6 oz trimmed fresh asparagus, chopped

⅔ cup dry white wine

⅓ cup arborio rice

freshly grated parmesan cheese (optional)

Serves 2

Asparagus and White Wine Risotto

Baby artichokes, fresh artichoke hearts and artichoke bottoms can all be cooked in the same way and make a delicious risotto, which can be served as a first course.

Melt half the butter in a heavy frying pan and gently fry the onion until softened. Meanwhile, bring the stock to a boil in a saucepan and drop the asparagus into it. Boil for 30 seconds, then strain the stock into a pitcher and refresh the asparagus under cold water. Mix the wine with the stock.

Stir the rice into the butter and onion, and when shiny with butter pour on a little of the wine/stock mixture. When this has been absorbed, pour on a little more and continue to cook gently until the liquid is again absorbed. Add the asparagus and a little more liquid. Continue cooking until all the liquid has been added and absorbed, the rice is creamy and the asparagus tender. When you are ready to serve, stir in the rest of the butter.

Freshly grated parmesan cheese can also be stirred into the risotto before serving.

COD FILLETS WITH BEET SAUCE

Skin the fish fillets and brush them all over with olive oil. Use the rest of the oil to grease an ovenproof dish. Lay the fillets flat in the dish. Crush the salt, pepper, garlic and seeds from the cardamom pods together and sprinkle this mixture over the cod fillets. Cover with foil or parchment paper.

Preheat the oven to 350°.

To make the sauce, heat the olive oil and gently fry the onion or shallots until softened. Add the celery, beet and the tomatoes, roughly chopped, and pour on the wine or stock. Bring to a boil and simmer, uncovered, until the vegetables are tender.

Meanwhile, bake the fish for 8 to 10 minutes. Add any cooking juices from the fish to the vegetables and boil to reduce the liquid a little. Keep the fish in a warm place until ready to serve it.

Blend the vegetables and liquid until smooth, then sieve into a clean pan. Reheat this sauce and season to taste. Spoon the sauce onto heated dinner plates, lay a fish fillet on top of each and garnish with some fresh chervil, coriander or flat-leafed parsley.

INGREDIENTS

2 thick fillets of cod, weighing 6–7 oz each

1 tbsp olive oil

salt and freshly ground pepper

1 garlic clove

2 cardamom pods

FOR THE SAUCE

1 tbsp olive oil

1 small onion or 2 shallots, sliced

½ celery stalk, sliced

¾ cup diced beets

¼ lb ripe tomatoes

⅔ cup white wine or Vegetable Stock

salt and freshly ground pepper

FOR THE GARNISH

fresh chervil, coriander or parsley

Serves 2

HEDGEROW SALAD
WITH WALNUT AND ARUGULA DRESSING

Wash the arugula leaves and drop into boiling salted water. Boil for 1 minute. Drain and squeeze dry. Put into a blender with the yogurt, walnut oil, garlic and seasoning to taste. Blend until smooth.

Arrange the salad leaves on large dinner plates, spoon the dressing on top and sprinkle with walnuts.

INGREDIENTS

¼ cup arugula

salt

½ tbsp thick plain Greek yogurt

1 tbsp walnut oil

1 garlic clove, chopped

freshly ground pepper

2 oz salad leaves (to include young dandelion leaves, chicory and lettuce as available)

1 tbsp chopped walnuts

Serves 2

LIGHT LEMON AND HAZELNUT SPONGE CAKE

INGREDIENTS

½ cup wholewheat self-rising flour

2½ tbsp raw brown sugar

2 large eggs

3 large egg whites

⅔ cup ground hazelnuts

grated zest of 1 lemon or
½ tsp lemon oil

FOR THE FILLING AND GARNISH

½ cup thick plain Greek yogurt

⅓ cup shelled hazelnuts

FOR THE SYRUP

1 tbsp clear honey

juice of 1 orange

juice of 1 lemon

Serves 4

Using wholewheat flour for this cake gives it an extra, and healthier, dimension. Contrary to expectation, it is light, moist and well risen. As it is difficult to make a small enough cake for two, have the leftovers for tea-time; because it is moist, the cake keeps very well until the next day. Unlike cream, the yogurt filling remains fresh-tasting and white.

This is an enormously versatile recipe; the flavoring and garnish can be changed according to season and occasion. Tia Maria flavoring and ground coffee garnish would make a more sophisticated version. A delicate flavoring of rosewater in the syrup could be enhanced by putting crystallized rose petals on top and adding minced fresh rose petals to the yogurt filling. A rum-soaked cake filled with bananas and yogurt would be rich, alcoholic and toothsome.

The mixture would also adapt to a jelly roll recipe, but if you do bake a sheet cake to roll up, don't scatter bran on the baking sheet first. The crunchy crust produced would make it very difficult to roll.

First prepare two 8 inch cake pans: cut two 8 inch circles of parchment paper and four 12 inch strips. Fit two strips into the bottom of each pan, in a cross. Lay the circles of parchment over them. Lightly oil the sides of the pans and the parchment.

Sift the flour into a bowl through a not very fine sieve. This will leave only the coarsest bran behind, but it will not be wasted. Sprinkle the bran evenly over the parchment paper in the pans. As the cake bakes, a lovely crust will form, and because much of the bran has been removed the cake will be better able to rise.

Preheat the oven to 400°.

Grind the raw brown sugar to powder in a coffee grinder. Crack the whole eggs into a mixing bowl, add the three egg whites and stir in the sugar. Beat with an electric mixer until the mixture is pale, frothy and much increased in volume. Carefully fold in the ground hazelnuts, sifted flour and grated zest of lemon – or use lemon oil instead of the lemon zest. Divide the mixture between the two cake pans and bake toward the top of the oven for 12 to 15 minutes.

Meanwhile, prepare the filling and the syrup. Stir the yogurt until smooth. Reserve a few whole hazelnuts for garnish and crush the rest; putting them in a paper bag and crushing with a rolling pin is the easiest method I know. Heat the honey gently and stir in the orange and lemon juices.

Remove the cakes from the oven and allow to rest for a few minutes. Ease the cakes away from the sides of the pans with your fingers or a knife then, using the strips of paper to help you, remove the cake layers from the pans and leave to cool on a wire rack, peeling off the parchment paper first.

For a simple gâteau, place one of the layers on a plate, sprinkle with a little syrup and spread the yogurt on quite thickly. Place the second layer on top and brush more syrup over the surface, covering it completely but reserving a tablespoon or so in the pan. Boil this until sticky, then brush on the edge of the cake in a 1 inch border. Sprinkle the crushed hazelnuts on the syrup border and garnish with the reserved whole nuts. For a more elaborate-looking cake, slice each layer into two, giving you three layers of filling.

Light Lemon and Hazelnut Sponge Cake

St Valentine's

DAY

On occasion I have taken the pink heart theme quite to excess with heart-shaped ravioli served with a pale tomato sauce, a salmon or smoked salmon dish, and *coeurs à la crème* served with rose-flavored syrup. And of course, presented it all on pink and white china, with a white cloth, lace and bows. What follows is a rather more sober celebration of the good saint's day, although I am not sure that Rosé Champagne Granita can ever be considered entirely "sober."

Like all good recipes, this one came about by accident and through a sense of thrift. Tom and I were working with a food photographer, putting together some dishes that go with Champagne. It was an entirely suitable job for us, since we have always felt that Champagne is a superb partner for many, if not most, foods. Bubbling glasses of Champagne also had to be shown in the picture. As every food photographer knows, the best way to put the fizz back in a glass of Champagne when it has been standing around on the set is to drop a pinch of sugar into it. However, we also had to have a photograph of Champagne actually being poured into a glass and, by the time the perfect photograph had been taken, the Champagne was tired and very sweet. As there was an awful lot of it, we couldn't bear to see it wasted so we took it home and froze it, and the granita followed. I have to tell you that, owing to a mistake on the part of the person supplying the Champagne, we were not using just ordinary rosé, but a magnum of Lanson rosé that had been in the cellars for some years and was a rare treat.

Some of our best dinner parties have been at the end of food photography sessions when the leftovers have been brought home and turned into imaginative combinations. Decorative vegetable garnishes can be tossed in butter or oil, herbs and garlic and stirred into pasta with a little goat cheese. Raw fish salads can be turned into fish soups.

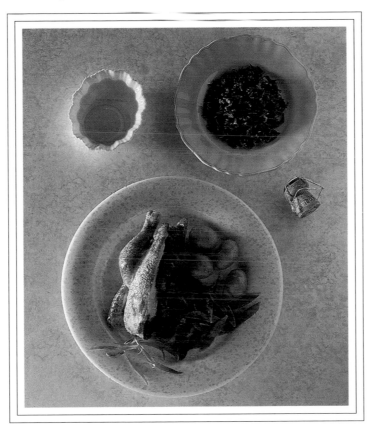

Mousseline of Scallop Roe
or
Scallops with Julienne of Vegetables

Stuffed Squab Chicken with
Vegetables
Wild Rice

Rosé Champagne Granita
Almond Cookies
or
Rose Hearts
Rhubarb Sauce

Sweetbreads with sorrel become ravioli filled with chopped sweetbreads and served on a pool of sorrel sauce.

My digression has taken us some way from our St. Valentine's day dinner. Whenever I can, I include some of my favorite dishes. Scallops are one of them – cooked in any style at all, even served raw. In fact, this is one of the most delicious raw foods imaginable. A good friend of ours and an excellent cook, Karin Perry, once served us scallops as good as I have tasted anywhere. She had diced them small, moistened them with a little hazelnut oil and served them with mâche (lamb's lettuce), concassé tomatoes and a little more dressing. It was fresh and delicate.

Scallop mousseline has a special place in my repertoire because it was just such a dish that I served to the judges in a cooking contest that I won, and from which date my career as a food writer can be said to have started. I do scallops in two equally delicious versions, the one given here with a saffron sauce and a pinkish mousseline and the original one, which has the scallops blended with cream, egg and a little saffron-flavored stock, with a sauce made from the coral blended with a little stock. Very gentle cooking is the secret here, to avoid a coarse texture to the mousseline. If it is easier for you to control, set the roasting pan or *bain-marie* on a low heat on the stove, covered with foil. I have also cooked similar dishes in an electric steamer quite successfully. For a simpler scallop dish, try the gently steamed Scallops with Julienne of Vegetables, which follows the recipe for the mousseline.

To follow this very delicate appetizer I have chosen a simple and robust main course: baby or squab chicken. I invented the recipe a few years ago when I was asked to create a menu for a meal to celebrate a French event. The meal had to be one that could be put together in an hour; I chose squab chicken, which is a good-tempered dish, as once it is in the oven you can get on with the rest of the meal. My appetizer was a smoked monkfish salad with pink grapefruit, and the dessert was meringues with chestnut purée. The main course has survived in my repertoire rather better than the others, whether I'm cooking it just for the two of us or for friends.

One of the many nice things about a dinner party for two is its intimacy and informality. So why not eat the chicken with your fingers? Some of the best dishes are to be eaten that way. I always think it a pity that at more formal dinners, especially abroad, "finger food" is banned. On a trip to Spain not long ago, I would have loved to have eaten the local seasonal specialties of quail and partridge when we were taken out to dinner, but it was simply considered unsuitable for guests to have to eat food with their fingers and instead we were served fillets of this and slices of that.

I have also included a recipe for cooking wild rice that would make a rather more unusual accompaniment to the chicken than new potatoes. It is expensive but, as you can see from the recipe, a little goes a long way. It is not really rice at all, but a wild grass that grows in the isolated lakeland area on the border between the United States and Canada. Harvesting the grass is labor-intensive: it is picked by hand by the local Indian population. Friends arriving from America always bring a few small boxes in their luggage for us, although it can sometimes be found here in specialist food stores. I had once thought that all wild rice was the same; it is not. I discovered this only after I had emptied several boxes into a large storage jar. Some of the grains are longer, some are darker, some definitely take longer to cook.

When I cook a celebration meal like this for the two of us, Tom will always serve Champagne. It does go with food quite splendidly. Of course, some Champagnes are better with a meal than others; we like to keep our Champagne for a year or two, as even the cheaper non-vintage wine benefits from this. For a treat we would serve one of the grander marques such as the Comtes de Taittinger, of which our favorite remains the now rather elderly yet stately 1975. Non-vintage Krug would be welcome too. If you make the Rosé Champagne Granita, save some of the Champagne to drink with it. For an accompaniment to the alternative recipe, Rose Hearts, see my note on demi-sec Champagnes on page 37.

TIMING

I would make the granita and the Almond Cookies in the morning, or even the day before. Simply remember to put the granita into the refrigerator at least half an hour before serving it to "ripen" it.

Get the chicken ready and put it in the oven and then make the scallop mousseline. The wild rice will need probably as long as the chicken to cook, and possibly more.

MOUSSELINE OF SCALLOP ROE

INGREDIENTS

½ lb sea scallops with large roes if
available, or 1 lb cleaned sea
scallops

1 egg

3 tbsp heavy cream

salt and freshly ground white
pepper

1 shallot, finely chopped

2 tbsp unsalted butter

⅔ cup Fish Stock

pinch of saffron threads

FOR THE GARNISH

fresh chervil or parsley

Serves 2

*Opposite: Mousseline of Scallop
Roe*

Preheat the oven to 300°.

If using whole scallops with their roe or coral, rinse them free of sand. Remove the thick pad of muscle and the roe. If you can't find scallops with roe, double the quantity of scallops (the resulting color will be whiter and the texture less grainy). Pick out two or three good scallops, slice them into rounds and set aside. Put the rest of the scallops, the roe (if using), egg, 2 tablespoons cream, and seasoning to taste in a blender or food processor and blend until smooth. Sieve.

Butter two small ramekins very well and set them in a roasting pan containing a little water. Fill the ramekins almost to the top with the scallop mixture. Place in the middle of the oven and cook for 25 minutes. The exact cooking time depends on the depth of the mixture: a knife point inserted in the center will come out clean when the mousseline is cooked.

To prepare the sauce, fry the shallot in half the butter until soft but not brown. Add the fish stock and boil to reduce by a third. Stir in the saffron and remaining cream and cook for 5 minutes. Strain and keep warm.

Quickly fry the sliced scallops in the remaining butter just before you are ready to serve the dish. Turn the mousselines out onto heated individual serving plates, mop up any liquid with a paper towel and surround each with a few spoonfuls of sauce. Lay the scallops on top of the sauce and garnish each slice with a tiny chervil or parsley leaf.

SCALLOPS WITH JULIENNE OF VEGETABLES

INGREDIENTS

6–8 plump sea scallops

1 garlic clove, crushed

1 in chunk fresh ginger root,
peeled and shredded

1 carrot, cut into very fine strips

1 leek, cut into very fine strips

1 celery stalk, cut into very fine
strips

salt and freshly ground pepper

½ lemon

2 tbsp Fish Stock

1 tbsp soy sauce

Serves 2

This is another way of serving scallops, either as an appetizer or as a main course.

Clean the scallops by rinsing thoroughly under cold water to wash away any sand. Remove the intestine and the thick muscle. Pat dry on paper towels and place in a shallow baking dish.

Scatter the garlic and ginger over the scallops, then heap the carrot, leek and celery on top. Season lightly. Squeeze on just a few drops of lemon juice and moisten with the fish stock and soy sauce.

Place the dish on an upturned saucer in a frying or sauté pan. Pour in 1 inch or so of water and cover with the lid or a sheet of foil. Bring to a boil and steam for 5 to 7 minutes, depending on how plump the scallops are and how well done you like them. Remove the scallops and vegetables and keep these warm on a serving plate. Slightly reduce the cooking juices and serve separately.

STUFFED SQUAB CHICKENS WITH VEGETABLES

INGREDIENTS

2 squab (baby) chickens weighing ¾ lb each

2 oz (4 medium slices) lean bacon

3 oz blood sausage or any good coarse pork sausage

2 slices of brown bread, crusts removed

2 sprigs of fresh French tarragon, if available, or ½ tsp dried tarragon

1 garlic clove, or more if you like, crushed

salt and freshly ground pepper

3 tbsp Cognac

¾ lb new potatoes, scrubbed

1 small head of lettuce

¼ lb snow peas or whatever fresh green vegetable is available

Serves 2

Squab or baby chickens are tender, juicy birds if properly cooked. Look for the smallest size available.

Cut the wing tips from the birds. Cut the bacon into narrow strips and cook it in a frying pan until most of the fat has been rendered.

Meanwhile, cut the sausage and bread into small cubes. Put these in a bowl. Lift the bacon from the frying pan with a slotted spoon and add to the bowl; reserve the bacon fat in the pan. Chop the fresh tarragon and add it to the bowl, with the garlic and a little salt and pepper. Moisten the stuffing with half the Cognac and stuff the chickens with the mixture. (It is much quicker to do this with your fingers than to fiddle about with a teaspoon.) Close the birds securely with wooden toothpicks.

Preheat the oven to 350°.

Heat the bacon fat in the pan and brown the chickens all over. Pour on the remaining Cognac and light it. When the flames have died down, transfer the birds to a casserole. Cover and cook in the oven for 35 to 40 minutes.

About 10 minutes before the chickens are done, put the potatoes on to boil. Remove any wilted leaves from the lettuce, wash it and shake dry. Roughly chop the lettuce, put it into the frying pan, moisten with water and quickly stir-fry until wilted. Cook the snow peas or other green vegetables for 2 to 3 minutes in plenty of boiling salted water; drain and refresh.

Serve the chickens on a small bed of lettuce, with the new potatoes and vegetables. Boil to reduce the cooking juices and serve as gravy.

WILD RICE

Two things strike me about this delicious cereal: how long it takes to cook and how much it increases in bulk. This quantity really is enough for two.

Put the rice in a saucepan and cover with water. Add a pinch of salt. Boil until the rice is tender – about 45 minutes to 1 hour. More water will be required during cooking, but it is impossible to say how much. Simply keep an eye on it to stop it drying out and burning.

INGREDIENTS

2½ tbsp wild rice

salt

Serves 2

Stuffed Squab Chickens with Vegetables

ROSÉ CHAMPAGNE GRANITA

INGREDIENTS

up to 1 tbsp confectioners' sugar, to taste

⅔ cup rosé Champagne

Serves 2

Extravagant but nice. It can be made with leftover Champagne, if there is such a thing.

Stir the sugar into the Champagne and freeze the mixture in a sorbetière or ice cream-maker, or in a freezerproof container in the freezer. If using the latter method, keep stirring the sides of the granita to the middle so that the mixture freezes evenly. A food processor is useful to blend the mixture before the final freezing.

Don't let the mixture freeze too hard. A granita is a soft, "grainy" mixture when it is served.

ALMOND COOKIES

INGREDIENTS

1 egg white

pinch of salt

¼ cup superfine sugar

½ tsp grated lemon zest

¼ tsp ground cinnamon

⅔ cup ground almonds

1 tbsp flour, sifted

Makes about 18

Crisp, delicate Almond Cookies contrast well with the Champagne Granita or any creamy dessert. Difficult to make in small quantities, they keep well in an airtight container.

Preheat the oven to 275-300°.

Whisk the egg white until foamy. Add the salt and continue whisking until firm. Gradually add the sugar and whisk until stiff. Carefully fold in the rest of the ingredients.

Line baking sheets with parchment paper and drop the mixture onto it in teaspoonfuls. Bake for 20 to 25 minutes or until set and golden brown. Cool on a wire rack.

Opposite: Rosé Champagne Granita with Almond Cookies

ROSE HEARTS

INGREDIENTS

⅓ cup thick Greek-style plain yogurt

¼ cup sieved cottage cheese

2 tsp rosewater

clear honey or sugar to taste

2 egg whites

Serves 2

This is a delicate, light dessert, considerably adapted from the traditional *coeurs à la crème*, which uses cream and cream cheese. Because of its light, mousse–like texture and ingredients this would not be appropriate to serve at the same meal as the Mousseline of Scallop Roes, but it would make a nice ending to the meal if you served the Scallops with Julienne of Vegetables to start.

You can serve Rose Hearts with a fruit compote, fresh fruit or a fruit sauce. At this time of year, a delicate pink sauce made from rhubarb is perfect (recipe below). In the summer or autumn, a soft fruit sauce is delightful. The flavoring of the yogurt and cheese mixture can also be changed: substitute orange flower water for the rosewater and serve with sliced oranges, or use freshly chopped mint for the rosewater and serve with black currant or raspberry sauce.

You can buy individual heart-shaped pierced molds imported from France in good kitchenware stores. Like much kitchenware, they are worth looking out for when you are in France as they are cheaper there. Line the molds with damp cheesecloth to stop the mixture drying out too much. If you cannot obtain molds, pierced yogurt or cottage cheese cartons are a good substitute, but you will lose the heart shape.

Blend the yogurt and cottage cheese, mix in the rosewater until smooth and sweeten to taste. Whisk the egg whites to form peaks and fold into the cheese.

Spoon the mixture into lined molds, place on a plate and refrigerate for about 12 hours to drain and firm up. When ready to serve, unmold onto plates and carefully peel the cheesecloth from the molded cheese mixture.

RHUBARB SAUCE

INGREDIENTS

¼ lb rhubarb

2–4 tbsp sugar to taste

grated nutmeg

Serves 2

Berry fruit sauces can be made following this method. Better still, if the fruit is very ripe, simply rub it through a sieve.

Chop the rhubarb into 1 inch chunks but do not peel it. Rinse it and place in a saucepan with the sugar. Cook gently, partially covered, until the sugar has melted and the fruit is tender. Rub through a sieve, sprinkle with nutmeg and chill until required.

DEMI-SEC CHAMPAGNES

When I worked in the south west of France as an *assistante*, my close friends in the small boarding school were the three *surveillantes* Michèle, Françoise and Nicole, and the assistant housekeeper Marie-Claire. The wine we normally drank with our meals was the rough red from Labastide de Lévis on the Tarn, but for *fêtes* and *anniversaires* we splashed out. Whoever was celebrating would go out and buy a bottle of Champagne and some pastries or *gâteaux secs*, which we would consume in mid-afternoon instead of our usual bowl of coffee. At the first such celebration I was shocked to discover that the Champagne was demi-sec. Even at the tender age of 21, I knew that one only drank dry wines; anything sweeter than brut was for the unsophisticated. Fortunately I quickly overcame my snobbery when I realized just how delicious this Champagne was, especially when served with almond cookies at teatime.

Tom and I now share a taste for this lovely wine, but sadly the occasions on which we drink it are all too rare because it is so difficult to find. Few Champagne importers keep it as they say there is no market for it. One or two brave souls stock it and so we encourage them by buying a bottle now and again. One of our greatest disappointments was at the Grand Véfour in Paris, now owned by Taittinger. We looked forward to choosing a demi-sec Champagne to go with our dessert only to be told that they kept none as it was completely out of fashion in France. Instead we were offered a muscat, admittedly delicious and currently extremely fashionable, but not at all the same thing.

A demi-sec Champagne would go very well with the Champagne Granita, or you might prefer to omit the granita and serve a demi-sec Champagne with the Almond Cookies alone. On the whole it goes best with *petits fours* or pastries, fruity desserts or a single piece of lusciously ripe fruit, such as a pear or a nectarine. It is rather less successful with chocolate desserts, but then so are most wines. Nor does it take well to rich, creamy, eggy sweets. However, I have to report that a highly successful marriage was made between a Lanson Demi-Sec and a special plum pudding I made. Unlike the usual, rich, dense mixture, heavy with dark fruit, this was a much lighter version using plenty of almonds, apricots and golden raisins. A foamy sabayon sauce to accompany it was made with a little of the Champagne.

DAYS

Rosemary, basil and tarragon all play their part in this meal full of fresh garden flavors, which would be wonderful to eat out of doors if you are lucky enough to have a garden or patio. "Outdoors" for us usually means moving our dinner table in front of the open window, from where we can enjoy our neighbors' gardens. Thyme and rosemary just about struggle through in my window boxes, lemon thyme in the north-facing one, common thyme and rosemary in the south-facing box. Thyme and rosemary flowers are my only crop. Apart from looking very fine as a garnish for salads, they are absolutely wonderful in soups.

Given the uncertainty of English summer weather, I long ago felt the need for soups other than the gazpachos, delightful though they are in their various tomato, almond and bean flavors. Such refreshing confections call for a still, fragrant night in a courtyard in Córdoba, not a gray, wet, summer evening in north London.

Michel Guérard's revolutionary (as it was then, some 15 years ago) combination of spinach and pears in a purée gave a hint as to a possible direction. The fruit enriched and filled out the vegetable flavor and texture but still remained only a hint in the background. Since then I have experimented with many combinations – carrot and apple, fennel and apple, tomato and red currant, zucchini and melon – and the soup recipes in this chapter are not very far removed from Michel Guérard's initial idea. The most successful soups have been those where the fruit and vegetable are complementary rather than hugely contrasting in flavor. And, of course, the colors must be similar; otherwise, if you cross a green vegetable with a red fruit, you finish up with a very muddy-looking soup.

The best thing about these soups is that they are equally delicious hot or cold. Although they will need stirring before serving, they do not have a great tendency to separate.

Carrot and Rosemary Flower Soup
or
Broccoli, Pear and Tarragon Soup
or
Tomato and Red Currant Soup
or
Tomato and Garlic Soup

Tomato, Basil and Cardamom Salad

Tarragon Pot-Roasted Quail
Warm Potato Salad

Apricots in Muscat Wine
or
Melon in Honey Ginger Syrup

One or two points common to the preparation of all of them need to be borne in mind. If you use a nonstick saucepan there need be no oily surface to the soup (and that means fewer calories). A vegetable stock or a very light chicken stock can be used. I prefer the former, as it does not mask the fresh flavor of the soup as a meat stock might. What's more, if the meat stock is too concentrated a chilled soup may well turn into a jellied one. Season the soup only lightly while hot and then, if serving chilled, add more seasoning if you think it needs it.

Chilled soups can have a spoonful of cream or yogurt whisked into them before serving. If you want to enrich a hot soup, break an egg into a small cup. Whisk in a tablespoon of hot soup and pour it through a sieve into the hot but not boiling soup and stir thoroughly. Chilled soups look particularly good served in glass bowls that have stood in the freezer for half an hour or so, and they should definitely be served cold rather than tepid.

Basil and tarragon are plants that need plenty of strong sunlight to develop and ripen the fragrant oils, which give them their flavor. Thank goodness for those strong, healthy basil plants to be found in my favorite Italian food stores. Either herb combines very well with tomatoes in a salad. A firm but ripe and perfumed tomato is one of my favorite summer things and we spend a great deal of time looking for good specimens. A pinch of sugar will help those who need it, as will some freshly ground cardamom. Your own home-grown tomatoes should need neither.

The quail can be served hot or cold, depending on the weather and the sort of meal you want to serve. They are also utterly delicious as picnic food. Simply wrap each of them in foil when cooled and pack up with the rest of the goodies. I remember a delicious accompaniment I once served with cold quail: mushroom sandwiches. Much easier to carry and eat than potato salad but serving the same purpose as a foil to the succulent meat, they could not be simpler to make. Cook mushrooms and a few pieces of chopped onion in butter until they are soft and all the liquid has evaporated. Cool and process with the same amount of butter, some salt and pepper. Spread the mixture on slices of bread, top with another slice and cut into four triangles, with the crusts removed for extra elegance.

For dessert I have suggested Apricots in Muscat Wine. Now it may be that you simply cannot get good ripe apricots, only pale, firm ones that have little flavor. In that case, poach them first in a little sugar and lemon syrup, then drain them and pour the wine over. Alternatively consider strawberries in Beaujolais, a delightful combination, or different types of melon scooped into balls and put into muscat wine or a honey ginger syrup. Peaches in hock are also delicious.

Which brings me to the wines to serve with this meal. Indeed a good hock would be excellent. I would serve an estate-bottled wine from the Rheingau for preference, of at least Kabinett quality, and possibly even a Spätlese. We are both firmly of the opinion that German wine is delicious with food, but realize that we are fighting a losing battle. As a completely contrasting alternative, a lightly chilled red wine would be excellent; young red wines react very well to chilling, which bring out the fruity and flowery qualities you want on this kind of day. A Chinon, a Bourgueil or a Saumur-Champigny, all French from the Loire valley, are ones that we love to drink.

TIMING

It is important when planning a summer meal to balance the temperatures. It is not a good idea to serve all cold dishes. Sometimes I serve a hot appetizer, a warm main course and a cold dessert, or I reverse that. For this meal serve the soup chilled or hot, nothing in between. The potato salad is best made a short time before serving it so that it is still warm. Dressings and vinaigrettes are absorbed much better when combined with warm vegetables. The quail should be served just tepid and should not, if possible, be refrigerated. If you have to do this, make sure you take them out at least an hour before eating to bring the flavors to life once more.

CARROT AND ROSEMARY FLOWER SOUP

INGREDIENTS

¼ lb carrots, sliced

1 shallot, chopped

1¾ cups Vegetable or Chicken Stock

1 small ripe peach

8 flowering heads of rosemary

salt and freshly ground pepper

Serves 2

The fruit is important in this recipe. You can't quite detect the peach flavor but it adds a certain richness to the soup.

Cook the vegetables until soft in a quarter of the stock. Allow to cool. Cut the peach in half, remove the pit and roughly chop the flesh. Put it in a blender or food processor with the carrot mixture, the rest of the stock and six of the heads of rosemary. Process until smooth. Chill.

Before serving, season to taste and garnish with the rest of the rosemary flowers.

BROCCOLI, PEAR AND TARRAGON SOUP

French tarragon is one of the most summery flavors imaginable. Take care to find the French variety, because the almost identical Russian tarragon is quite bitter and does not lend the same, sweet aniseed flavor.

Trim the scallions of their roots and of most of their green tops, which you put aside. Chop the onions, the broccoli and the pear and put in a nonstick saucepan with the tarragon, keeping a few tarragon leaves back for garnish. Add 1 cup of the stock and cook gently until the broccoli is tender. Add the scallion tops once you have removed the pan from the heat. Pour half the remaining stock into a blender or food processor, add the cooked vegetables and fruit and process until smooth. Sieve and stir in the rest of the stock. Season with nutmeg, salt and pepper, and finish off as appropriate according to whether you are serving the soup chilled or hot. Garnish with the reserved tarragon leaves.

INGREDIENTS

4 scallions
½ lb broccoli florets
3 oz ripe pear, cored but not peeled
2 sprigs of fresh French tarragon
3¼ cups Vegetable or Chicken Stock
pinch of grated nutmeg
salt and freshly ground pepper
cream, plain yogurt or beaten egg to enrich, depending on whether you are serving the soup chilled or hot (optional)

Serves 2 (plus leftovers)

TOMATO AND RED CURRANT SOUP

Red currants and tomatoes make a marvelous combination, but you could also try strawberries (not too ripe) as an alternative to the currants.

Peel and thinly slice the onion. Cook in a nonstick saucepan until soft and translucent. Quarter the tomatoes, strip the red currants from their stems and add both to the pan. Pour on a quarter of the stock and simmer gently for 10 minutes until the red currants and tomatoes have softened. Stir in the sugar.

Remove the pan from the heat and allow to cool. Rub the cooked fruit and vegetables through a sieve and stir in the rest of the stock. Season to taste, then chill the soup and serve garnished with fresh basil or mint leaves.

INGREDIENTS

1 small onion
225 g (8 oz) ripe tomatoes
75 g (3 oz) ripe red currants
300 ml (10 fl oz) Vegetable or Chicken Stock
good pinch of unrefined sugar
salt and freshly ground pepper

FOR THE GARNISH

fresh basil or mint

Serves 2

Opposite: Carrot and Rosemary Flower Soup

TOMATO AND GARLIC SOUP

INGREDIENTS

1 onion, thinly sliced

2 large heads of garlic

2½ cups Vegetable or Chicken Stock

large pinch of ground ginger, or ½ in cube fresh ginger root, peeled and chopped

1 lb ripe tomatoes, roughly chopped

salt and freshly ground pepper

cream, plain yogurt or beaten egg to enrich, depending on whether you are serving the soup chilled or hot (optional).

Serves 2 (plus leftovers)

Here is a soup for those who are not yet quite convinced that tomatoes and red currants together make a delicious soup. The amount of garlic required is not a misprint. When cooked, garlic has a mild rather than pungent flavor. If you can find them, use fresh plum tomatoes for their firm sweetness.

Sweat the onion in a nonstick saucepan until softened. Add the separated garlic cloves, which you do not need to peel. Pour on a quarter of the stock, add the ginger, cover with a lid and cook gently until the garlic is soft. Then add the tomatoes, stalks, skin, seeds and all, and cook for just 2 or 3 minutes.

Rub the mixture through a sieve and mix with the rest of the stock. Season lightly and serve hot or chilled, enriched if you wish.

TOMATO, BASIL AND CARDAMOM SALAD

Thinly slice the tomatoes. Remove the seeds from the cardamom pods, crush them and scatter over the tomatoes. Tear the basil leaves into small pieces rather than chop them – this seems to retain the flavor better. Sprinkle the basil on the tomatoes and drizzle the oil over. Tomatoes have their own natural acidity and need no vinegar. Lightly season with salt and pepper and allow to stand for at least 1 hour before serving to allow the flavors to develop.

NOTE ON SALAD DRESSINGS

Not all salad ingredients are as easy to dress as sweet, ripe tomatoes, which need little to enhance their unique fragrance and flavor. I have already mentioned the array of oils and vinegars I keep in my kitchen pantry (page 11) and I cannot overemphasize how valuable they are. Clearly others have recognized this too. We no longer have to go to France to buy hazelnut and walnut oil as supermarkets now import it for us, and it is readily available in America. If I am using one of these expensive oils I will put little else with it – just a splash of very good vinegar, a little freshly ground black pepper and some sea salt. A clove of garlic might well also be crushed and added to the salad bowl.

If you happen not to have any very good oil on hand, or if you have a particularly bland salad to dress, perhaps my secret weapon might help. It is part of a highly unorthodox vinaigrette which nevertheless draws compliments from the most discerning. The secret weapon is ketchup.

Mix ½ teaspoon Dijon-style mustard with ½ teaspoon ketchup and a splash of soy sauce in the bottom of a large salad bowl. Add a splash of Angostura bitters and one of Worcestershire sauce. Season with salt and freshly ground pepper, then gradually stir in olive oil or grapeseed or sunflower oil. Add the washed, dried salad leaves. Turn until well coated and serve.

INGREDIENTS

½ lb firm but ripe tomatoes

8 cardamom pods

12 large leaves of fresh basil

2 tbsp extra virgin olive oil

salt and freshly ground pepper

Serves 2

Tomato, Basil and Cardamom Salad

TARRAGON POT-ROASTED QUAIL

INGREDIENTS

2 or 4 quail, depending on
   appetite

1 tbsp soy sauce

½ tbsp good olive oil

1 shallot, finely chopped

6 sprigs of fresh French tarragon

5 tbsp dry white wine

salt and freshly ground pepper

Serves 2

Squab (pigeon) and squab chickens can be cooked in the same way. For them, increase the cooking time to 45 minutes.

Trim and tie the quail neatly if they have not already been trussed. Rub them all over with the soy sauce and let them stand for 30 minutes or so.

Preheat the oven to 350°.

Heat the olive oil in a small flameproof casserole and fry the shallot without browning it. Strip the leaves from the tarragon; break each stem into three or four pieces and place inside the cavity of the birds. Fry the quail with the shallot until browned all over. Add most of the tarragon leaves (saving some for garnish) and the wine and bring slowly to simmering point, then cover the casserole and transfer to the oven. Cook for 25 minutes.

When they are cooked, place the quail in a shallow china dish. Strain the pan juices over the birds, season lightly and garnish with the reserved tarragon leaves.

WARM POTATO SALAD

INGREDIENTS

¾ lb new potatoes

salt

dressing (see recipe text)

Serves 2

Other warm vegetable salads can be made in exactly the same way. Carrot flavored with thyme, and green beans with raw mushrooms are just two that I like.

Scrub the potatoes but do not peel them. Drop them into boiling salted water and boil until just tender. Drain them and toss while still hot in your favorite salad dressing, perhaps a nut oil vinaigrette, a yogurt, garlic and chive mixture, or light cream mixed with black pepper and chopped chervil.

Opposite: Tarragon Pot-Roasted Quail, Warm Potato Salad

APRICOTS IN MUSCAT WINE

INGREDIENTS

6–8 ripe apricots

⅔ cup muscat wine

Serves 2

Prepare this at least a day before required. Peaches, nectarines and sweet gooseberries are also delicious treated in the same way.

Cut the apricots in half and twist away from the pit. Place the halves in a glass dish and pour the muscat wine over the apricots. Cover and chill. The soaked fruit is very good served with the Almond Cookies on page 34.

MELON IN HONEY GINGER SYRUP

INGREDIENTS

2 tbsp clear honey

¼ cup water

juice of ½ lemon

1 in chunk of ginger root, peeled fresh or crystallized

2 cups mixed melon balls

Serves 2

For an attractive-looking dish use two or three different types of melon with different colored flesh: cantaloupe, Crenshaw, honeydew.

Put the honey, water and lemon juice in a saucepan and bring to a boil. Slice the ginger, cut it into thin strips and add them to the syrup. Cook for 2 or 3 minutes, allow the syrup to cool then pour it over the melon. Serve chilled.

Opposite: Melon in Honey Ginger Syrup

By the Sea

This entire meal reminds me of one we ate with friends in northern Norfolk in England. They knew that the region was quite unfamiliar to us, so served a procession of local delicacies, beginning with Great Yarmouth crabs. They were freshly steamed and fragrant, needing nothing more than melted butter in which to dip the juicy morsels of crab meat. These were followed by a large bowl of glasswort, which was a completely new treat for us; we did not know what to do with it. We were shown how to hold a branch by its roots, dip it in yet more melted butter and suck the green fleshy parts from the stems, a little like eating asparagus or artichoke leaves. I have included a recipe for glasswort, also known as samphire, because it fits in so well with the rest of the meal. However, it is not something for which I can offer a substitute should you be unable to find it; there is simply nothing in the world quite like it. In summer (it is, I must emphasize, a truly summer flavor), when we have an abundance of it, either brought by friends from Norfolk or purchased at considerable expense in London fishmongers, I like to prepare it in different ways. It is excellent stirred into hot pasta with a few shrimp or clams, and delicious as a salad; but you could use it instead of vegetables in my recipe for crab and vegetable quiche. It is also wonderful with potatoes in a Spanish omelette, and it can be pickled in a sweet spicy vinegar to serve with raw fish salads in winter.

While picking crab out of the shell might be the easiest way of eating the meat, it is also the messiest. You might prefer to get the mess over with in advance by cleaning the crab and then using it in a quiche or an omelette. For some reason eggs go very well with crab. Think of crab soufflés. Think of homemade ravioli, made with eggs, stuffed with crab. Here I combine it with whatever fresh young vegetables are available and bake it in a light custard quiche.

You will imagine yourself by the sea – even if you are

Crab and Vegetable Quiche

Glasswort with Lemon Butter

Turbot with Laver Sauce
Mixed Lettuce Salad

Strawberries with Honey and Balsamic Vinegar
or
Jellied Muscat Mold

not – once you smell and taste the iodine-rich sea vegetables called laver I have suggested for the turbot. Sometimes, in Wales, where laver is traditionally served, it is made into a sauce, mixed with a little orange juice, to accompany lamb. It is also mixed with oatmeal and fried in bacon fat as a breakfast dish – laverbread. But for me, it goes best of all with fish. A little goes a long way. It is a rich dark purée of concentrated seaweed flavors that I like to thin down into a sauce made with the cooking juices. I have also used it as a pasta stuffing and, indeed, colored and flavored homemade tagliatelle with it to serve with a shellfish sauce. You can find it sometimes at fishmongers or, canned, in specialty food stores.

This meal seems to demand a salad rather than a cooked vegetable. For those with their own vegetable patches, what could be nicer than to pick a few fresh leaves from different varieties of lettuce? One year I managed to grow lettuce in my window box – the small leaf variety from which you can take just a few leaves rather than having to use the whole head.

Do not imagine that the Strawberries with Honey and Balsamic Vinegar is a modish, "nouvelle-ish" whim. This is a classic preparation in Modena, the home of balsamic vinegar, and the condiment is well worth keeping in your pantry. In the next chapter I show how it can be used in savory sauces. It is also excellent in salad dressings of expensive nut oils. As it is made from fermented grape juice rather than oxidized wine it is milder than wine vinegar and has a subtle yet distinctive flavor of its own.

Muscat grapes are beautifully aromatic and delicious eaten on their own at the end of the meal. An old-fashioned jellied mold is a more unusual alternative and the recipe could not be more simple.

A crisp, refreshing wine is what we would serve with such a meal. To start with, if such a thing were available here, a half bottle of fresh fino sherry would be perfect. Very few are exported, which is sad since that is how the folk of Cadiz and Jerez drink fino, sharing a half bottle as an appetizer wine or apéritif. Another crisp refresher that would go well with all the fishy, complex flavors is a Sauvignon Blanc. A Sancerre or Pouilly Fumé would be fine but these are rather expensive and, dare one say it, somewhat overrated. We would tend to look for a Fumé Blanc from California or Australia. From France, the Sauvignon de St. Bris is hardly to be bettered for its scented, "flowering currant" nose. It has never reminded me of gooseberries (with which it is often associated); black currants, perhaps, but flowering currants most of all.

TIMING

The strawberries need to sit in their marinade for a while, so prepare these first. Otherwise all the dishes are last-minute preparations, with the exception of the crab quiche. This can be prepared much earlier, although it is best served warm.

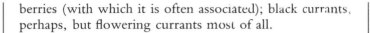

CRAB AND VEGETABLE QUICHE

INGREDIENTS

pie pastry to line an 8 in quiche dish

6 oz (about 1¼ cups) white crab meat

1¼ cups cooked diced vegetables

3 large eggs

1 cup milk

grated nutmeg

salt and freshly ground pepper

Serves 2 (plus leftovers)

You can make one large tart, for which I give the recipe here, two individual ones, or a dozen small ones, which make good snacks to serve with drinks.

For me the food processor is absolutely indispensable when it comes to making pastry. I once found myself in a Parisian cookery school, having a go at making a pâte brisé. The chef in charge came over to see how I was getting on, seized my hands and shook his head pityingly. I have hot hands, which melt the fat in the pastry mix long before it gets to the oven. Choux pastry is no problem and, of course, my hands are not a handicap when it comes to molding hot-water pastry over a jam jar to make pork pies. For the rest I use a food processor and iced water, and am not ashamed to admit to buying frozen pastry on occasion.

Regarding the crab meat, you can of course buy it ready-prepared, but because it is so labor intensive it will be very expensive. If, however, you are going to clean your own crab you need to look for one that is heavy for its size, which means that it has plenty of meat. Shake it and listen; it should not sound watery.

The crab you buy from a fish market may be already cooked. This is how to get into it. First, twist off the legs and claws, crack them, and extract all the white meat contained in them. Place the crab on its back and pull the body away from the shell. Behind the head is the grayish-white stomach sac which should be discarded, together with the feathery gray gills, the "dead men's fingers." Crack the body part and remove the white meat, a skewer or lobster-pick being the best implements.

Preheat the oven to 375°.

Roll out the pastry and use to line an 8 inch fluted quiche dish. Prick the pastry all over. Put the dish on a baking sheet and bake blind for 10 minutes. Remove from the oven and allow the pastry case to cool.

Arrange the crab meat on the bottom of the pastry case and scatter the vegetables on top. Beat the eggs, milk and seasonings together and pour onto the filling. Bake in the oven at 350° for 25 to 30 minutes. This quiche tastes best warm, neither hot nor cold.

Opposite: Crab and Vegetable Quiche

GLASSWORT WITH LEMON BUTTER

INGREDIENTS

¾ lb glasswort

unsalted butter

juice of ½ lemon

freshly ground black pepper

Serves 2

Opposite: Glasswort with Lemon Butter

This is best cooked as simply as possible. It is eaten in the fingers like asparagus, which could be served with this lemon butter if you can't find glasswort.

Thoroughly wash the glasswort in several changes of water, and either scrub the root systems or remove them. Place in a saucepan, cover with boiling water and cook, covered, for up to 10 minutes or until tender. Alternatively it can be steamed. Drain.

Melt as much or as little butter as you want and stir in the lemon juice and black pepper.

Serve the glasswort on a large plate or in a bowl and hand the lemon butter separately.

TURBOT WITH LAVER SAUCE

INGREDIENTS

1¼ cups Fish Stock or unsalted court bouillon

2 turbot fillets, weighing 6 oz each

1 tbsp laver or nori

1 tbsp unsalted butter

salt and freshly ground pepper

Serves 2

Of course, any fish fillet can be used in this recipe; it doesn't have to be turbot.

Pour the stock or court bouillon into a frying pan and lay the fish fillets in it. Bring slowly to just below simmering point and poach the fillets for 2 to 3 minutes. Remove with a slotted spatula and keep them, covered, in a warm place.

Raise the heat and boil to reduce the stock by three-quarters. Stir in the laver or nori and butter until thoroughly blended. Season to taste. Spoon onto heated dinner plates and arrange the fish fillets on top.

2

STRAWBERRIES WITH HONEY AND BALSAMIC VINEGAR

INGREDIENTS

1½-2 cups strawberries

3 tbsp balsamic vinegar

1 tbsp clear honey

Serves 2

A simple dish such as this needs no further garnish or flavor.

Slice the strawberries into a glass dish. Mix the balsamic vinegar and honey and pour over the strawberries. Chill for 1 to 2 hours, and serve on chilled plates.

JELLIED MUSCAT MOLD

INGREDIENTS

1 envelope unflavored gelatin

1¼ cups unsweetened grape juice (bottled or carton)

4 scented geranium leaves, washed and dried (optional)

about 1¼ cups large muscat grapes, peeled and seeded

Serves 2

Opposite: Strawberries with Honey and Balsamic Vinegar

Aromatic muscat grapes are grown in California. Use white grape juice with white grapes and red or purple juice with dark grapes. The flavor is deliciously "grapey."

Soften the gelatin in a little grape juice. Heat ⅔ cup of the juice and stir in the softened gelatin and the juice until the former has dissolved. Pour, with the remaining juice, into a bowl and allow to cool.

When cool, spoon a shallow layer into the bottom of a dampened mold or individual molds and refrigerate. When almost set, lay in the leaves, veined side uppermost. Refrigerate again to set completely.

Cut most of the grapes in half. Place a layer of grapes on the set gelatin and pour on some more liquid, continuing until all the fruit and liquid are used up. Chill until set.

To serve, unmold onto individual serving plates and decorate as you wish.

Summer

From all our travels we bring back mementos. Sometimes it is photographs we look at to remind us of a particular place. More often, it will be recipes that have been given to me directly by the people who have cooked the dishes for us, or that I have re-created as closely as possible to the original. Then, of course, I begin to add my own touches and it is no longer possible to say that that is the original shellfish dish from Brittany or that the original pasta dish from Emilia Romagna.

The Almond Soup here is, however, still very closely related to the bowl of Gazpacho Blanco we tasted during a visit to southern Spain some years ago. Before that visit I had thought there was only one gazpacho, the tomato and olive oil-based Gazpacho Andaluz. In fact there are three, the third made of beans.

When you don't want to spend hours over a hot stove, calf's liver is one of the best choices for a main course. It is readily available at all times of the year, which is useful, but for a hot dish in summer it is perfect. Quick cooking of this delicacy is essential if you are to retain its tender pink center. (If you do not like liver, then why not try cooking a thin fillet of salmon or sea trout – or the Lamb Fillet on page 66 – in exactly the same way?) I do more of my cooking on a gas burner than in my electric oven and thus am quite happy to have a couple of pans on the go, one for the calf's liver and one for a stir-fry of vegetables. This is a marvelous way of cooking vegetables to retain their color and crispness, thus providing a perfect foil for the liver.

Kissel is a superb recipe for the soft berry fruits of summer and autumn. It has a clear, limpid, jewel-like color and a cool, smooth, refreshing texture and flavor. It needs to be prepared well in advance to enable it to set and chill. I was taught how to make this by a lady in whose house we rented an attic flat for many years. She was a critical teacher but was finally satisfied with my kissels. She also

Almond Soup
or
Gazpacho Andaluz

Calf's Liver with Sage
and Balsamic Vinegar
Stir-Fried Green Vegetables
or
Lamb Fillet
with Basil and Sauvignon Sauce
Broccoli with Tomato and Soy Butter

Cherry Kissel
or
Clafoutis

taught me to make borsch, another of her specialties; this I often cook in winter as a rich meal in a bowl. In summer I strain it and serve it chilled and sometimes jellied – but not at the same meal as kissel because they look similar.

The kissel is a typical Russian dessert: the French would be more likely to present the cherries in a Clafoutis – a more substantial, rustic dish, usually served at room temperature but nonetheless wonderful eaten cold for breakfast the following morning.

Dolcetto, that light red wine from Piedmont in Italy, would be a perfect accompaniment to the main course. Dolcetto d'Alba and the hard to find, because consumed locally, Dolcetto d'Ovado both have a curious hint of almonds that reflects the soup. Asti Spumante is a much-despised white sparkler: all the more for us! At its best it has a lovely fruity flavor, redolent of the heady muscat grape from which it is made. It is perfect with many of the fruit desserts in this book, and is delicious on its own or with a fresh peach and a handful of macaroons.

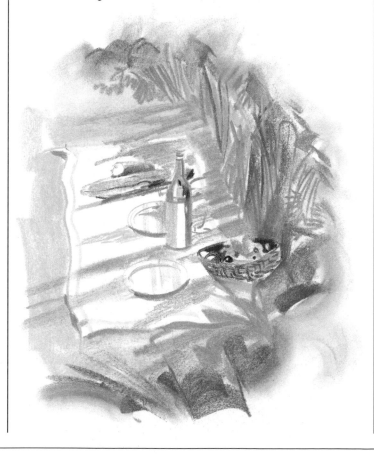

ALMOND SOUP

We first tasted this dish in Córdoba, in a lovely courtyard at the restaurant El Churrasco. The use of almonds in cooking comes from the Moorish period of Spanish history, when the first almond trees were planted. Always use sweet almonds in this recipe. Bitter almonds have a stronger flavor, which would not be suitable. It is always preferable to buy the freshest whole almonds available. To skin them, put them in a bowl, pour boiling water over them, leave for one minute and then drain. Rub them between your fingers to peel them, allow them to cool and then grind them.

To start the soup place the ground almonds in a bowl and pour on the boiling water. Let the almonds soak overnight, covered, in a cool place. When ready to serve, stir in the stock, the olive oil, garlic and seasoning to taste. If the soup needs chilling further, add a couple of ice cubes. Serve in individual bowls, and pass the garnishes separately.

INGREDIENTS

4 heaping tbsp ground almonds

⅔ cup boiling water

1¼ cups Chicken or Vegetable Stock

2 tsp extra virgin olive oil

2 garlic cloves, crushed

salt and freshly ground white pepper

FOR THE GARNISH

peeled and halved grapes

raisins

small croûtons

finely diced apple tossed in lemon juice

Serves 2

Almond Soup

GAZPACHO ANDALUZ

INGREDIENTS

½ lb very ripe tomatoes

slice of bread 1 in thick, crusts
    removed

1 garlic clove, crushed with ¼ tsp
    salt

2–3 tbsp extra virgin olive oil

2 tbsp red wine or sherry vinegar

2 scallions, chopped (optional)

chilled water

TO SERVE

diced cucumber

diced, peeled and seeded tomatoes

croûtons

Serves 2

Gazpacho is a lovely, refreshing soup for which there are
many, many recipes. I make it without sweet peppers.

Roughly chop the tomatoes on a plate so that all their juice is
conserved. Crumble the bread into a bowl and add the garlic
and the chopped tomatoes. Stir in the olive oil, vinegar and
scallions. Cover and refrigerate for 1 hour to allow the flavors
to develop.

   Put in a blender or food processor and process until
smooth. Add chilled water to give about 2½ cups liquid.
Strain and serve in chilled bowls with the accompaniments
handed separately.

CALF'S LIVER WITH SAGE
AND BALSAMIC VINEGAR

INGREDIENTS

1 tbsp flour

1 tsp fine sea salt

1 tsp freshly ground pepper

pinch of ground ginger

pinch of ground allspice

½ lb calf's liver

2 tbsp unsalted butter

sprig of fresh sage

2 tbsp balsamic vinegar

Serves 2

Put the flour, salt, pepper and spices in a strong paper bag and
shake to mix. Cut the liver into two pieces and shake each one
in the bag of seasoned flour.

   Melt half the butter in a heavy frying pan and when hot add
the pieces of liver. Fry quickly on both sides until golden; 2 to
3 minutes altogether should cook it to pink. Give it longer if
you prefer it well done. Remove the liver and keep it warm.

   Add the rest of the butter to the pan with the sage leaves
and the balsamic vinegar. Heat together, stirring, to make a
light sauce. Serve the liver, with a little of the sauce and a sage
leaf or two, on heated dinner plates.

*Opposite: Calf's Liver with Sage
and Balsamic Vinegar*

LAMB FILLET WITH BASIL AND SAUVIGNON SAUCE

INGREDIENTS

10 oz lamb fillet, cut from a rack of lamb

2 garlic cloves

1 tsp Dijon-style mustard

1 tbsp olive oil

⅔ cup Sauvignon Blanc

5 tbsp Light Meat Stock

several sprigs of basil (at least 12 good-sized leaves)

salt and freshly ground pepper

Serves 2

For those who are not fond of liver, here is a delicious, tender alternative that is very quickly cooked on the top of the stove in the same way as the calf's liver. By the summer months the price of "spring lamb" has come down considerably although it is still a young, delicate meat. A white wine sauce enhances this rather more than might a red, and you should consider serving the same wine with it, perhaps an inexpensive Sauvignon de Touraine, the pricier Sauvignon de St. Bris or a Sancerre. Alternatively, look for one of the lovely California Sauvignon Blancs.

Trim the lamb of most of its fat. Peel and slice the garlic and cut into thin slivers. Insert these into the meat at intervals. Mix the mustard, olive oil and a tablespoon of wine and brush over the meat. You can prepare it to this stage and refrigerate, covered, for several hours or overnight in order to let the flavors develop.

Slice the fillet into 4 or 6 rounds and flatten them slightly. Heat a well seasoned or a nonstick frying pan and when hot place the sliced fillet in it, in a single layer. Sear on one side, then lower the heat for 1 to 2 minutes. Raise the heat and turn the meat over, searing the other side, then cook for a few minutes on a lower heat. How long you cook it will depend upon the thickness of the slice of meat and how rare or well done you enjoy your lamb.

Remove the meat and keep it covered in a warm place while you make the sauce. Raise the heat under the frying pan and pour in the rest of the wine. Let it bubble fiercely while you scrape up any residue cooked to the bottom of the pan – which should not happen with a well seasoned or nonstick pan, but even the most careful cooks burn their pans from time to time.

Pour on the stock and let the liquid reduce to 4 or 5 tablespoons of good, rich gravy. Shred the basil leaves and add these, together with whatever seasoning you feel the sauce requires. Serve with the lamb on heated dinner plates, perhaps with your favorite potato dish or with Broccoli with Tomato and Soy Butter. It will be equally good with Stir-Fried Green Vegetables.

BROCCOLI WITH TOMATO AND SOY BUTTER

This dish, with a slightly oriental touch both in its method of cooking and in its flavors, is good enough to serve on its own as an appetizer. It would be ideal to serve to vegetarians.

Break the broccoli into florets and peel and slice the stalks on the diagonal to give a large cooking surface. Bring a pan of water to a boil with the sesame oil and salt. Drop in the broccoli, bring it back to a boil, keep boiling for 30 seconds then drain and plunge the broccoli into chilled water, or at least rinse it well under the cold tap to cool it quickly.

In a wok or frying pan, heat the water or stock with the soy sauce and vinegar. Add the broccoli, cover and steam it until just tender. Remove the broccoli and keep it warm over hot water, leaving the cooking juices in the frying pan or wok.

Add the diced tomato and quickly reduce to a couple of tablespoons or so of tomatoey liquid. Turn off the heat, add the cubes of butter one at a time and whisk into the sauce until it emulsifies and thickens. Season with a little white pepper. Extra salt should not be required because of the salt content of the soy sauce. Serve the sauce and broccoli separately or together, as you wish.

INGREDIENTS

½ lb broccoli

1 tsp sesame oil

2 tsp salt

2 tbsp water or Vegetable Stock

1½ tbsp soy sauce

½ tbsp sherry or rice vinegar

1 tbsp peeled, seeded, diced tomato

2 tbsp unsalted butter, chilled and cubed

freshly ground white pepper

Serves 2

STIR-FRIED GREEN VEGETABLES

INGREDIENTS

½ in chunk of fresh ginger root

2–3 garlic cloves

1 oz snow peas

1 oz scallions

1 oz thin green beans

1 oz broccoli florets

1 oz mushrooms

1 oz baby corn

1 tbsp peanut oil

1 tbsp soy sauce

2 or 3 drops of sesame oil

Serves 2

Choose the vegetables according to season. If some require more cooking than others then start them first, adding the others in the order of how long they take to cook.

Peel the ginger and garlic and cut into thin slivers. Prepare the vegetables as appropriate. Substitute others if any of those suggested are not available. Heat the peanut oil in a large frying pan, add the vegetables and cook, stirring, until tender but still bright and crisp. Moisten with the soy sauce and cook for a further 1 to 2 minutes. Serve sprinkled with sesame oil.

CHERRY KISSEL

Since we have very little choice when we come to buy cherries, simply look for the largest, brightest, freshest you can find. Kissel can also be made from autumn fruits such as blackberries, blueberries or cranberries, in exactly the same way.

Wash the cherries and remove the stalks and pits. Place them in a blender or food processor with half the water. Process for 3 to 4 seconds, then strain the liquid through a fine sieve into a bowl and set aside.

Put the residue from the sieve in the remaining water in a saucepan, bring to a boil and cook for 5 minutes. Strain the liquid into a clean pan and stir in the sugar until dissolved. Bring to a boil. Stir in the potato flour, previously dissolved in a little cold water. Add the first batch of berry juice and bring the mixture back to a boil, stirring continuously. Boil for 2 minutes only, then pour the mixture into a glass bowl and chill. (It is important not to boil the mixture for more than 2 minutes or it will begin to thin down again.) Serve when cold and set, with a little cream or plain yogurt.

INGREDIENTS

1½ cups ripe cherries

1¼ cups water

2½ tbsp raw brown sugar

1 tbsp potato flour

TO SERVE

light cream or yogurt

Serves 2

CLAFOUTIS

One traditional French recipe I have adopted is Clafoutis, and it is now firmly in my repertoire, both as a sweet and as a savory dish. Plumped-up dried apricots, prunes pitted and soaked in tea or red wine, or good apples, peeled and sliced, would all make good substitutes if cherries are not available. Cubes of cheese and anchovies can be used to make a savory version.

Preheat the oven to 350°.

Thickly butter a 10 inch or 12 inch fluted quiche dish with half of the butter. Place the fruit on the bottom. Make a batter of milk, flour, eggs and sugar and pour over the fruit. Dot with the remaining butter, and sprinkle with a pinch of nutmeg or cinnamon – or a mixture of both if you wish – and bake in the oven for about 45 minutes or until puffy and golden brown.

Remove from the oven and expect the clafoutis to sink slightly. It has a fairly solid texture, not a light delicate one. Serve warm, with cream or *crème fraîche* if you prefer.

INGREDIENTS

4 tbsp unsalted butter

2 pints cherries, washed and pitted

2 cups milk

½ cup + 1½ tbsp flour

3 large eggs

½ cup sugar

grated nutmeg and ground
  cinnamon

TO SERVE

Cream or crème fraîche (optional)

Serves 2 (plus leftovers)

Opposite: Stir-Fried Green Vegetables

Harvest

FESTIVAL

To me autumn means beans – lots of them, in all varieties, from the pink speckled borlotti to the pale green flageolet and the black bean so good cooked with bacon. Beans are one of the finest ingredients I know for soups and casseroles such as cassoulet and even chili con carne; I feel they are indispensable to this hot, spicy meat mixture, although there are those who maintain that the dish is correctly prepared without beans. Most delicious of all are the bean soups of Europe, the fabada Asturiana from northern Spain and the ribollita of Tuscany being the best in my view. The latter is the second-day version of the Bean and Vegetable Soup given here.

If you are cooking the white navy or cannellini beans, make more than you require and save a portion for the next day. You can then make a simple appetizer by opening a can of tuna fish, mixing it with the beans, some extra virgin olive oil and thinly sliced onion rings. Yes, canned tuna fish. With tomatoes and anchovies, tuna is one of the few canned items allowed in my pantry.

Autumn is also about game. I love to cook game in all its forms, from a quickly roasted wild duck or grouse to a slowly cooked casserole of elderly pheasant. While most of the feathered game is wild or undomesticated, some game – such as rabbit and quail – is being farmed. On the one hand, this is to our advantage because it is available for much longer, but on the other hand, it takes away all the anticipation and enjoyment of a seasonal treat.

I often cook venison steaks or medallions as it is possible to buy just enough for two, rather than a whole roast. It is a lean and relatively healthy meat. Breasts of pheasant or squab can be cooked in the same way as the recipe here, and make a useful, quickly prepared dinner. Autumn and winter vegetables partner them very well, and I have given recipes for two of my favorites: a sweet, crunchy Fennel Salad and a Celeriac and Potato Cake.

Bean and Vegetable Soup
or
Bean and Pasta Soup

Medallions of Venison
Marinated in Pomegranate
Celeriac and Potato Cake
Fennel Salad

Pears and Fresh Ginger
in Spiced Red Wine Syrup
or
Caramel Pears

Pomegranates are surpringly successful as a marinade for venison; for my taste they have just the right amount of acidity. So often the use of lemon juice or orange juice in a marinade is overdone to the point when it interferes with the wines. It is also useful to find a marinade that does not require wine. (In this meal I have chosen to keep the wine for the pears.)

And how I love autumn fruits. Out come the jam kettles at this time of the year just as if I had a large farmhouse kitchen. I scour Hampstead Heath for blackberries and pester our local Greek greengrocer for quinces. Happily I have long passed the stage of scrumping from neighbors! During October, I find making a few jars of plum jam, a batch of wild bramble jelly, and even rows of garnet Quince Jelly (recipe on page 80), quite irresistible if I am given some. Crab apples and medlars can be found in our urban streets as well as in country gardens, and these make some of the finest jellies. Even cooking apples are useful as a basis for excellent herb-flavored varieties. All are extremely easy, follow the same basic principles, and are just as well worth making in small quantities as large ones. Apart from being nice small gifts for Christmas, they are excellent with game dishes, making all the difference to, for example, the medallions of venison.

Apples and pears also go beautifully with the rich spicy flavors I like in autumn. Pears in wine with spices is one of my favorite standby dishes. Sometimes I cook them in left-over sweet wine, sometimes in white wine, but I particularly like their color when they are cooked in red wine. If you do not have or do not like ginger, try the delicious spice combination of cinnamon and cardamom instead. The alternative recipe, for Caramel Pears, requires no addition of wine – the fruit is cooked in butter, sugar and its own juice.

With the rich, robust food I like in autumn, rich, robust wines are called for – ones that you can metaphorically stand a spoon up in, as you can in the ribollita. The best Bartolos and Chiantis are one suggestion, but Riojas would also be in keeping. Otherwise you could try a Shiraz from Australia or one of those big "blackberry-ish" Zinfandels from California.

Our friends in San Francisco who keep our pantry well supplied with wild rice and blue corn are also very concerned to show us the best of California's wines. On their last visit, they brought a bottle of 1984 Lytton Springs Zinfandel from Sonoma County. It was a magnificent wine.

To accompany it I made a steamed venison dessert, a variation on the steak and kidney dessert theme, in which I used stout instead of red wine. The combination was perfect.

TIMING

The bean soup requires lengthy cooking, so allow 2 hours to include preparation. The venison is not cooked until the last minute but needs to be placed in the marinade at least an hour before, or even the preceding day. The vegetables can be prepared in advance, but are cooked just before serving. Because both pear recipes are served chilled they are cooked earlier and left in the refrigerator until required.

BEAN AND VEGETABLE SOUP

INGREDIENTS

½ cup dried navy or cannellini beans

1 tbsp olive oil

1 medium onion, chopped

1 celery stalk, diced

1 large carrot, diced

2 zucchini, sliced

a few green beans if available

14 oz can tomatoes

3½ cups Vegetable or Light Meat Stock

1½ oz uncooked spaghetti

2–3 garlic cloves, crushed

fresh basil, chives or parsley

extra olive oil

Serves 2 (plus leftovers)

Start preparing the beans the day before required. Cover them with cold water, bring very slowly to a boil and boil them fast for 15 minutes. Drain, rinse and place in a large bowl. Cover well with boiling water and let them soak overnight, or for at least 6 hours; drain.

Meanwhile prepare the vegetables. Heat the olive oil in a heavy saucepan and fry the onion, celery, carrot, zucchini and green beans without browning them, but until they smell good. Rub the tomatoes through a sieve over the vegetables. Add the stock and the rinsed beans. Bring slowly to a boil, then cover and simmer for 1 to 1½ hours.

About 20 minutes before serving, break up the spaghetti and add to the soup, together with the garlic. When the spaghetti is cooked, shred the fresh herbs, stir them in and serve the soup in deep, heated soup bowls. Float a little olive oil on the surface.

To serve the next day: toast 2 slices of bread and place them in soup bowls, pour on a little olive oil and pour the boiling soup over the bread.

BEAN AND PASTA SOUP

INGREDIENTS

1 onion, chopped

2 garlic cloves, crushed

4 ripe tomatoes, peeled and seeded

1 tbsp olive oil

3½ cups Vegetable or Light Meat Stock

1 heaping cup cooked navy or cannellini beans, or canned cannellini

2 oz dried pasta

salt and freshly ground pepper

½ tbsp pesto (optional)

Serves 2 (plus leftovers)

Opposite: Bean and Vegetable Soup

Here is a particularly delicious and satisfying soup (the combination of the beans and the grain in the pasta provides first-class protein). It is a good way of using up cooked beans from another dish, but is well worth making from scratch, too.

This soup can be made in many versions, adding zucchini, turnip, watercress and celery to turn it into a meal in itself, to be accompanied by good crusty bread and a glass of wine, with some fresh fruit to follow.

Cook the onion, garlic and tomatoes in the olive oil for a few minutes. Pour on the stock, bring to a boil and reduce by about a third. Pour a little of this mixture into a blender, add a quarter of the beans and make a purée. Add this and the rest of the beans to the pan and bring back to a boil. Add the pasta and cook until it is *al dente* (firm to the bite). Season to taste and stir in the pesto if you have it; this does add a lovely flavor to these rich robust soups.

MEDALLIONS OF VENISON
MARINATED IN POMEGRANATE

INGREDIENTS

2 medallions of venison, weighing
   5 oz each

1 large ripe pomegranate

grated nutmeg

⅔ cup Light Meat Stock

salt and freshly ground pepper

Serves 2

Noisettes of lamb or small filet mignons can be cooked in the same way.

Trim any fat and sinews from the meat. Cut the pomegranate in half. Remove some of the seeds for garnish and squeeze the rest on a lemon squeezer. Strain the pomegranate juice over the venison, sprinkle on some nutmeg, and marinate for at least an hour, and overnight if you wish.

   Remove the meat from the marinade and dry it thoroughly; reserve the marinade. Heat a nonstick frying pan and when hot put in the venison. Cook on a high heat on both sides until it reaches the right stage of cooking for you. Remove and keep warm. Add the stock and marinade to the pan and reduce to a few tablespoons. Season to taste and spoon the sauce onto heated dinner plates. Place the venison on top and garnish with the reserved pomegranate seeds.

CELERIAC AND POTATO
CAKE

INGREDIENTS

1 potato, weighing ½ lb

1 chunk of celeriac, weighing ½ lb

salt and freshly ground pepper

2 tbsp unsalted butter

Serves 2 (plus leftovers)

Peel and par-boil the vegetables. When they are cool enough to handle, shred them on a grater or in the food processor. Mix together and season with salt and pepper.

   Melt half the butter in a small frying pan and press the vegetable mixture into it. When cooked and brown on one side, slide it onto a plate. Melt the rest of the butter and cook the celeriac cake on the other side until golden brown. Cut a wedge for each serving.

*Opposite: Medallions of Venison
Marinated in Pomegranate*

FENNEL SALAD

You can, of course, vary the dressing you use on this salad. Nut oils are very good with fennel.

Remove any bruised part from the fennel and trim off any discolored bits, then slice thinly. Stir the oil, orange juice and seasoning together and pour over the fennel.

1 fennel bulb

2 tbsp extra virgin olive oil

1 tbsp fresh orange juice

salt and freshly ground pepper

Serves 2

PEARS AND FRESH GINGER IN SPICED RED WINE SYRUP

INGREDIENTS

2 or 4 pears, depending on size

2 in piece of fresh ginger root

2 tbsp honey

juice of 1 orange

1 cup red wine

grated nutmeg

Serves 2

Look for ripe but unblemished fruit. Any pear variety will do. A few slivers of toasted almonds are good sprinkled on the pears, which can also be served with cream or plain yogurt.

Peel the pears with a potato peeler and place them in a heavy saucepan. Peel the ginger, shave off thin slices with the potato peeler and lay them among the pears. Mix the honey with the orange juice and the red wine. Pour over the fruit, sprinkle with nutmeg, cover and poach gently for 20 to 30 minutes or until the pears are tender.

Carefully remove the pears and place them in a dish. Boil up the wine syrup and reduce by half. Pour over the pears. Allow to cool, then chill and serve.

CARAMEL PEARS

INGREDIENTS

2 good, evenly shaped pears

2½ tbsp sugar

2 tbsp unsalted butter

⅔ cup heavy cream

Serves 2

Opposite: Pears and Fresh Ginger in Spiced Red Wine Syrup

Here is an even richer way of cooking pears.

Peel the pears, keeping the stalks on. In a heavy pan, allow the sugar to melt over a very low heat. Add the butter, then the pears. Cook slowly until the pears are soft but not breaking up. During the cooking the pears will give off some of their juice and you will have a good syrup.

Remove the pears from the buttery syrup with a slotted spoon. Reduce the syrup a little and add the cream. Bring to a boil and let it cook for 3 to 4 minutes, when it will turn to a rich, warm, caramel color. Remove from the heat. Pour over the pears and serve cold.

QUINCE JELLY

INGREDIENTS

2 lb quinces

7½ cups water

juice of 1 lemon

sugar (see method)

Makes about 3 pints jelly

Fruits such as quince make lovely, firm, jewel-like jellies. Two extracts can be taken – that is, the fruit pulp, once boiled, can be boiled up again with fresh water in order to obtain the maximum from the fruit. Black currants and red currants can be treated in the same way. Blackberries cannot, and only one extract can be taken. Make the jelly in large enough quantities for you to keep some and give some away.

Chop the fruit quite small after wiping it all over and place it in a large saucepan with two-thirds of the water and the lemon juice. Simmer very gently until the fruit is tender. Quinces are hard and take much longer to cook than berry fruits or even apples – at least an hour, I usually find.

Scald a jelly bag or a large piece of cheesecloth and pour the fruit pulp into it. Allow the pulp to drip through for 15 minutes and then return it to the pan with the rest of the water. Simmer for a further 30 minutes and strain it once again. Do not squeeze the pulp in an attempt to encourage it to drip more quickly – it will only make the jelly cloudy.

Measure the juice and pour it into a large saucepan together with about 2 cups sugar per 2½ cups juice. Bring the sugar and the juice to boiling point and boil rapidly for 10 to 15 minutes until jell point is reached. Test for this by dropping a teaspoonful onto a cold saucer. When the jelly is cold it will set.

Remove the jelly from the heat, let it stand for 15 minutes and skim off any foam. Pour into small heated jam jars, which have been thoroughly washed, cover with a waxed disk and top with a cellophane cover.

ROSEMARY JELLY

At this time of year apples and crab apples are abundant. I can remember as a child rows and rows of jars of crab apple jelly; because it was so plentiful, it was no longer a delicacy. How I would love to have a few jars of it in my pantry now.

Apple jelly on its own is not particularly exciting but it provides an excellent base for more unusual flavors. I particularly like to make herb jellies, which are excellent served with meat, game and poultry. Herbs have no properties that lend themselves to jelly making, except for their flavor of course, and so need a pectin-rich vehicle with a fairly neutral flavor and color. Rather than use bottles of commercial pectin, I prefer to use apples. I have given a recipe for Rosemary Jelly, but all the herbs with distinctive flavors and plenty of essential oils, such as thyme, sage and tarragon, work well. I have not been able to capture the true basil flavor, and I am certain that chervil would not be very successful. My most exciting jelly has been the one I make during the summer with lavender; if there are no early apples available, I use rhubarb as the base.

To make Rosemary Jelly, wash the apples. Cut into chunks and put in a large saucepan, together with six of the rosemary sprigs. Cover with water and simmer until the apples are tender and pulpy. Strain the pulp through a jelly bag without squeezing or forcing, otherwise the jelly will be cloudy.

Measure the liquid and add 2⅓ cups sugar for each 2½ cups liquid. Strain the lemon juice into a saucepan and add the apple juice and sugar. Tie four sprigs of rosemary in cheesecloth and add to the pan. Bring to a boil and boil fast for 10 minutes or until jell point is reached (which is when a drop of syrup will set on a cold saucer).

Remove the cheesecloth bag of rosemary and pour the jelly into sterilized jars. Add an extra sprig of rosemary to each jar for identification, seal and label.

INGREDIENTS

4 lb apples

10–15 sprigs rosemary, each 3 in long

juice of 2 lemons

sugar (see method)

Makes about 3 pints jelly

Winter

WARMER

The inspiration for some of the dishes in this meal comes from Germany. One winter we arrived in Stuttgart and were about to embark on a hunt for "new" German food, but we needed to go no farther than the suburbs of the city where we found the delightful Schlosshotel Leonberg, owned and run by the Faeckls. Franz was a fine, imaginative chef who served local ingredients and recipes with an immensely delicate touch. Thus his oxtail stew was succulent and full of flavor without being fatty; he had also removed the bones. I now prepare my oxtail in a similar way and use the bones to make an extra portion of stock. This really is one of the finest winter dishes you can make, and it remains inexpensive. An alternative way of using oxtail is as a first course in a lovely, rich, tasty terrine that you can serve with just a few salad leaves or, for a more substantial dish, with a lentil salad.

There is a danger in food writers making statements about value for money. I once made a comment about brill (a flat fish) being good value when I gave a recipe for it in my weekly column, and not only could I not find any left in the stores when I went out to buy some that same Saturday, but I now notice there is very little difference in price between brill and turbot for which it was so long, and so wrongly in my view, considered a cheap substitute in Britain. The fish recipe I have suggested here as an appetizer uses a method more often found in restaurants than in the domestic kitchen, but it's great fun to cook and serve food in paper parcels and then watch your guests' enjoyment as they cut them open for themselves, appreciating the good scents of food that waft toward them. Meat, fruit and vegetables can also be cooked thus. Of course, whatever you cook should have a neat, smooth shape: a fillet or a slice of something is better than, say, a whole fish or chicken or anything with bones or spikes to pierce the paper. It is also important to remember that any seasoning

Flounder with Celery, Leeks and
Tomatoes

Chilled Rhubarb Soup

Oxtail Stew
Thimble Dumplings

Lemon Rice Pudding
or
Green Fruit Salad

or flavoring must go into the parcel at the beginning. This is not like a casserole where you can adjust the seasoning as you go along, but the great advantage of the method is that all the flavors, scents and cooking juices stay right there with the fish in the parcel.

And so to the rhubarb soup. It is one of those brilliantly simple ideas that you kick yourself for not having thought of first. At least I do. I long to serve elaborate, lengthy dinners in January and February just as an excuse to include it. Simply chilled, it makes a wonderful change from the sorbet served between fish and meat courses. Also, it is one of the few dishes that is actually complemented by the ubiquitous and rather awful kiwi fruit; the colors and tart flavors work happily together.

After the Oxtail Stew, the Lemon Rice Pudding as I have given it can be served hot or cold. It can also be turned very quickly into a chilled soufflé. Do this by separating an egg and stirring the yolk into the hot dessert. Whisk the egg white until it is stiff, fold this into the mixture and spoon the dessert into ramekins. Rice dessert is one of those delicious dishes to cook when you have the oven on anyway, and one which I too rarely remember. The Green Fruit Salad makes an easy and refreshing alternative.

There is no question about the wines Tom and I would drink with this meal: they would be German. With the fish we would drink a glass of Baden wine, which is drier than those from further up the Rhine valley, but still fresh and flowery. With the oxtail we would choose between a spicy, fairly full white wine from the Rheinpfalz and one of those hard-to-find German reds, a Weissherbst made from the Pinot noir grape (known in Germany as the Spätburgunder), or even one of the Würtemberger wines such as the Trollinger.

TIMING

Much will depend on whether you serve the rice dessert hot or cold. If cold, you can prepare it, like the oxtail, the day before. The fish can be prepared, put in its paper parcel and kept in the refrigerator for a couple of hours before you cook it. I would make the rhubarb soup the morning before required. If you leave it overnight in the refrigerator you must be very careful to cover it hermetically so that it does not absorb any refrigerator flavors and smells. However, it does tend to lose its freshness quite quickly.

FLOUNDER WITH CELERY, LEEKS AND TOMATOES

Fillets from other flat fish can be cooked in this way, as can slices from the thicker fillets of round fish such as salmon and trout.

Cut two sheets of parchment paper, each 15 × 10 in. Fold each sheet of paper in half and cut it into a heart shape with the fold down the middle. Lightly butter the paper. Skin the fish fillets and trim them into a neat shape.

Preheat the oven to 350°.

Trim the stringier bits from the celery, cut the stalk into three and then thinly slice each piece into julienne strips. Cut the leek in two or three pieces, then cut in half and finally into shreds. Wash the celery and leek thoroughly, then blanch them in boiling water for 30 seconds. Drain and refresh under cold water. Drain again.

Spoon half the diced tomato on each paper heart, to one side. Lightly season the fish fillets, fold them and place on top of the tomatoes. Pile the vegetable julienne on top, moisten with a little wine or stock and sprinkle with herbs. Seal the parcels by folding the edges tightly together and twisting the two ends.

Lay the parcels on a baking sheet and bake for 8 minutes. Serve immediately on heated dinner plates, each of you opening the parcel with a small knife or with scissors.

INGREDIENTS

4 fillets from a flounder weighing about 1 lb
1 celery stalk
1 leek
1 medium-sized ripe tomato, peeled, seeded and diced
salt and freshly ground pepper
1 tbsp white wine or Fish Stock
1 heaping tsp chopped fresh parsley, chives or scallion

Serves 2

Flounder with Celery, Leeks and Tomatoes

OXTAIL TERRINE

INGREDIENTS

¾ lb cooked oxtail, off the bone

4 small leeks or 2 larger ones

4 small carrots or 2 larger ones

salt and freshly ground pepper

up to 2 cups cooking juices (made
from cooking oxtail with wine
and pig's foot)

½ tsp dill seed

Serves 4 to 6

When you are making the Oxtail Stew (overleaf) it is worth buying extra oxtail, cooking it, degreasing it and removing it from the bone to make a jellied terrine to slice and serve as a rustic first course. The aspic will be all the better if you have cooked a chopped-up pig's foot with the oxtail.

Cut the meat into small dice. Cut the vegetables in half, or quarters if thick ones are used, and steam or boil in salted water until tender; drain.

Place some of the meat on the bottom of a 5 × 4 × 3 inch loaf pan. Arrange the leeks on top, then add more meat, the carrots and a final layer of meat. Season the cooking juices with salt and pepper to taste, add the dill seeds and pour over the meat. Chill until set, then unmold and slice.

CHILLED RHUBARB SOUP

INGREDIENTS

¾ lb trimmed rhubarb, cut into
chunks

1¼ cups water

½ vanilla bean

1 tbsp sugar, or according to taste

Serves 2

For garnish, I suggest a few slivers of kiwi fruit whose flavor perfectly complements that of rhubarb.

Place the rhubarb in a saucepan with the water, vanilla bean and sugar. Cover with a lid and stew very gently until the rhubarb is soft. Remove the vanilla bean and put to one side. Strain the mixture through a scalded cheesecloth or very fine sieve into a bowl. Taste and sweeten a little more if necessary, but bear in mind that the finished soup should be refreshing to the palate and thus still quite sharp. Scrape a little of the vanilla seed into the liquid, stir it and chill thoroughly before serving.

Opposite: Chilled Rhubarb Soup

OXTAIL STEW

INGREDIENTS

1 lb oxtail

1 small onion, sliced

2 garlic cloves, crushed

⅔ cup good red wine

½ tsp dill seed

½ tsp chestnut flour or potato flour

1 tsp blueberry or cherry jam

salt and freshly ground pepper

2 tsp slivovitz, malt whisky or kirsch

Serves 2

It is important to remove as much fat as possible from this dish at every stage. It transforms a fairly humble dish into something quite sumptuous.

Tiny new potatoes go well with Oxtail Stew if you don't want to make dumplings. Also consider broccoli florets, and slices of carrot that you've first carved with a cannelling knife – a small tool for cutting grooves out of vegetables; when sliced you have a flower shape. Steam the carrots and broccoli for 5 minutes only.

Chop the oxtail into chunks if the butcher has not already done so. Trim as much fat as possible from it and fry until well browned in a nonstick frying pan. Transfer to a casserole or heavy saucepan.

Fry the onion in the frying pan until just browning, add the garlic and fry together for 30 seconds. Pour on the wine and add the dill seed. Cook for another 30 seconds, then pour over the oxtail. Cover and barely simmer for 2 hours.

Remove the oxtail from the sauce. Cool it rapidly, cover and refrigerate it overnight. Do the same with the sauce, sieving it first.

Next day separate the meat from the bone and scrape the fat from the sauce. Place the meat and sauce in a pan and heat slowly. Mix the flour with a little water and stir into the stew. When it has thickened slightly, add the jam then season to taste. About 5 minutes before serving, pour in the spirit; the alcohol will have evaporated by the time you serve the dish.

THIMBLE DUMPLINGS

INGREDIENTS

½ cup cottage cheese

1 egg yolk

2 tbsp unsalted butter, melted

2 egg whites

1 heaping tbsp self-rising flour

1 tbsp fresh bread crumbs

Serves 2

Put the cottage cheese, egg yolk and half the butter in a food processor and process until smooth. Whisk the egg whites until stiff and fold into the mixture, then sprinkle on the flour and fold in. Dust with more flour if necessary to make the dough easy to handle.

Roll out on a floured board and cut into ½ inch chunks. Roll the chunks into balls and make a depression in each with your finger.

Drop the dumplings into boiling water and cook for 15 minutes. Fry the bread crumbs in the rest of the butter and roll the drained dumplings in them.

Opposite: Oxtail Stew, Thimble Dumplings

LEMON RICE PUDDING

INGREDIENTS

2½ tbsp short-grain rice

1¼ cups whole milk

thinly peeled zest of 1 lemon

2 cloves

seeds of 4 cardamom pods

1 tbsp sugar

juice of 1 lemon

TO FINISH

a little cream (optional)

ground cinnamon or grated nutmeg

Serves 2

Until we started eating desserts like this in Portugal, I had always thought of rice dessert as a nursery dish. Not a bit of it; it goes down very well with demanding guests.

Preheat the oven to 350°.

Put the rice, milk, lemon zest, cloves, cardamom seeds and sugar in an ovenproof dish. Cover and bake in the bottom of the oven for 1 to 1½ hours or until the rice is tender and creamy.

Remove the cloves and lemon zest. Stir in the lemon juice, and taste to see if more sugar is required. If the mixture is too stiff for your taste, add a little cream. Spoon into small rame-kins and lightly dust with cinnamon or nutmeg.

GREEN FRUIT SALAD

INGREDIENTS

1 lb of a mixture of the following:

muscat grapes

sultana or Thompson grapes

green apples

green pears

star fruit (carambola)

melons

a few spoonfuls of fruit juice

FOR THE GARNISH

twists of lime

passion fruit seeds

Serves 2 (plus leftovers)

Sometimes, even in the middle of winter, a sharp, refreshing finish to the meal is what you want rather than a soothing, rib-sticking dessert. Here is something easy to make – simply a mixture of all the good green and yellow fruit you can find, home grown and imported. Eat any that is left for breakfast.

Peel, deseed, core, pit and slice the fruit as appropriate and serve it in a glass bowl with a few spoonfuls of good fruit juice for the syrup (apple and pear are nice and clear) and a few twists of lime and some passion fruit seeds for decoration.

Opposite: Lemon Rice Pudding

Christmas

DINNER FOR TWO

We usually spend Christmas Day with family or friends, and so our own quiet celebration is likely to take place on Christmas Eve. It will be a late dinner or supper, perhaps followed by a walk around our London village to stand outside all the churches in turn and listen to their Christmas Eve carols.

Each year I try to devise a menu that will combine unusual ideas with traditional ones. Shellfish and smoked salmon are familiar hors d'oeuvres at a Christmas feast, and so I have presented them in new guises. After those fishy appetizers, it is good to freshen the palate with a tingling sorbet in preparation for the main course. A goose or a turkey would overwhelm a table for two. These are to be kept for occasions over the holidays when you might be doing some large-scale entertaining. Instead I might do partridge or a small Roast Duck – a perfect size for two people – or, perhaps more unusually, roast beef, albeit a small piece. I chose to break with tradition completely for the dessert in this menu and selected Chilled Persimmon Creams. The colors in the food – orange golds, vermilions and scarlets – are the rich colors of the Christmas season. Although this menu was designed with Christmas festivities in mind, it is, I am sure you will agree, flexible enough to be used for other celebrations.

Cold salmon canapés are delicious followed by hot oysters. The recipe for Oysters in Spinach Overcoats will, I hope, be recognized by my good friend Clare, who is an excellent cook. She and James served us these delectable morsels at a winter dinner party once, just two or three on a plate, crisp and hot on the outside, juicy and oystery on the inside. Mussels, shrimp (even mushrooms for those who do not like shellfish) can be cooked in this way. The recipe for Turkey Filo Pastry Pie on page 102 makes use of the remaining filo pastry from the Oysters in Spinach Overcoats, and is perfect for a larger gathering.

Smoked Salmon Shapes

Oysters in Spinach Overcoats

Sicilian Orange Sorbet

Roast Beef Tenderloin
or
Roast Duck
or
Pot Roast Partridge
Rice Stuffing
Baked Jerusalem Artichokes

Broiled Radicchio and Goat Cheese

Chilled Persimmon Creams
or
Mincemeat Soufflé

Roast Beef Tenderloin is something I rarely cook for the two of us as it is not really practical to cook a small piece. One answer is to cook a large roast and "resign" yourself to lots of luxurious sandwiches, or trim off a few slices before you marinate and cook it. Place these in plastic wrap and roll them out as if you were rolling pastry. This flattens them better than beating them, which is likely to cause them to tear. Then you can arrange the slices, trickle on a little extra virgin olive oil and garnish with a little grated parmesan cheese, a few leaves of arugula or thinly sliced celery or fennel; thus you have carpaccio, that very popular and expensive Italian appetizer.

It was in restaurants in Trieste that we first came across radicchio cooked in many ways – fried, broiled, in risottos and in pastas. I almost like it better this way than raw; it gains a nutty flavor in the cooking process. Goat cheese complements it admirably.

When I first planned this meal I had not thought of it as an Italian one, but Italian fruits do come to us at this time of year. Sweet oranges from Sicily – now called ruby oranges instead of blood oranges so as not to offend our delicate sensibilities – make marvelous juice for the best Mimosa in the world, and for a very delicious sorbet to eat after the fish and before you start on the main course.

For an unusual yet simple dessert, Chilled Persimmon Creams is one of my favorites. True persimmons are an extraordinary fruit. We rarely see them in perfect condition, which is when they are absolutely ripe, translucent, swollen and fragile. Greengrocers are, of course, reluctant to sell them like that and instead buy and sell them under-ripe. They look wonderful, an unblemished golden orange fruit, but if you eat an unripe persimmon you will encounter a mouthful of tannic, mouthpuckering flesh. Instead, wrap them in newspaper or brown paper, keep them in a warmish kitchen and only eat them when they have reached that perfect ripeness. (The Sharon fruit variety from Israel can be eaten at any time as they do not have the same amount of tannin in the skin.) Incidentally, the tannin and the pectin in persimmons make them ideal for jam-making. One December I made, for presents, small jars of cranberry and persimmon jam. Delicious on toast or scones with cream, it also has enough acidity to serve with a pale, delicate meat such as chicken or turkey.

For those who like a more traditional dessert, I have also included a recipe for a Mincemeat Soufflé that is quick and simple to make.

A celebration calls for Champagne and that is what we would drink as we prepared this meal, me cooking it, Tom arranging the table. This is when we would bring out one of our older Champagnes, or one of those non-vintage bottles bought on special offer that we then put away and forget about for a year or two. The main wine would be a claret, possibly from the ready-to-drink 1976 vintage, perhaps a soft, velvety St. Julien, a Léoville Barton or a Château Gloria; or perhaps a Pauillac such as the Lynch Bages, which is made of rather sterner stuff. With either Chilled Persimmon Creams or a tropical fruit salad, we would probably choose a half bottle of one of those lovely flowery orange muscat wines from California or Australia, equally delicious with the Mincemeat Soufflé.

TIMING

Take your time and be fairly relaxed about this meal. The canapés can be prepared well in advance and kept in the refrigerator. The cold ones can be eaten while the hot ones are cooking. Make the sorbet and the cream the morning before required and put the beef in to roast at the same time as the oysters. You can in fact cook them at the same temperature, the beef higher in the oven than the oysters. Otherwise, put it in after the oysters have cooked, and take longer over the meal.

SMOKED SALMON SHAPES

INGREDIENTS

4–6 slices of good fresh brown bread

2 tbsp unsalted butter, softened

¼ lb smoked salmon

FOR THE GARNISH

thin slices of lemon

fresh dill fronds

Serves 2

You could use a flavored butter or cream cheese under the smoked salmon, but on the whole I think this fish needs to be accompanied by only the simplest ingredients.

Trim the crusts from the bread. Spread with softened butter and lay the smoked salmon on top. Trim to fit the slices exactly; I find this can be most neatly done with kitchen scissors. The trimmings can be used as a garnish for another dish, or stirred into scrambled eggs for a special breakfast.

Then, with pastry cutters of different shapes, cut out the canapés. Alternatively, simply cut into triangles, squares or fingers. Garnish with tiny slivers of lemon and fronds of dill.

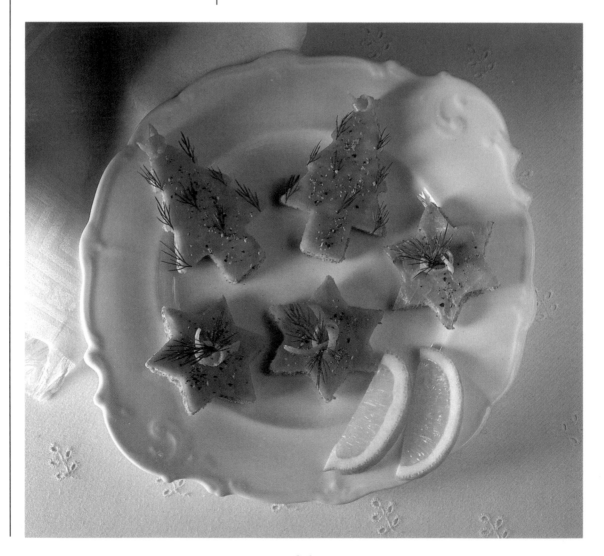

OYSTERS IN SPINACH OVERCOATS

If fresh oysters are not available, you can use frozen oysters and cook them without thawing.

Cut each sheet of pastry into 4 strips and pile them one on top of the other on a damp dish towel. Wrap the towel around the pastry to prevent it from drying out.

Remove the central rib from the spinach leaves and blanch them by draping them over a colander and pouring boiling water over them. Refresh under cold water and dry them carefully. Wrap each oyster carefully in a spinach leaf, lightly seasoning with salt and pepper and a drop of lemon juice.

Preheat the oven to 400°.

Unwrap the pastry and brush the top strip with some of the melted butter.

Place a wrapped oyster at the bottom right hand corner of the strip, i.e. the edge nearest you. Fold the pastry over the oyster so that the bottom edge now meets the left hand side, to form a triangular shape. Now fold that triangle over so that the parcel is sealed, and continue folding over until the strip completely encloses the oyster in a triangular parcel. Place on a baking sheet. Make the other parcels in the same way. Bake for 8 to 10 minutes.

INGREDIENTS

3 sheets of filo pastry
12 medium spinach leaves
12 raw oysters
salt and freshly ground white pepper
juice of ½ lemon
2 tbsp unsalted butter, melted

Makes 12

*Opposite: Smoked Salmon Shapes
Left: Oysters in Spinach
Overcoats*

SICILIAN ORANGE SORBET

INGREDIENTS

1¼ cups freshly squeezed orange juice

⅔ cup sugar syrup, made by boiling one part sugar with two parts water

1 tbsp orange flower water

Serves 2 to 4

Ruby-fleshed blood oranges give a lovely color and are worth searching out.

Stir the liquids together and freeze either in an ice cream-maker or sorbetière according to the directions of the manufacturer, or in a freezerproof container in the freezer. If using the latter method, the mixture will require stirring from time to time to break up the ice crystals.

It is a good idea to do the last "stirring," when the mixture is quite well frozen, in a food processor.

ROAST BEEF TENDERLOIN

A fillet of lamb (cut from the rack or rib), veal or venison can be cooked in the same way. The last two will require basting as they are dry meats with no internal marbling of fat.

Trim the beef of any fat, membrane and gristle. Mix together the rest of the ingredients, except for salt and pepper, pour over the meat and leave overnight in a cool place.

Preheat the oven to 425°. Remove the meat from the marinade, which you strain and reserve, and dry thoroughly on paper towels. Heat a nonstick frying pan and sear the meat all over. Transfer to a small roasting pan and roast in the oven for 20 to 30 minutes, depending on how rare you like the meat. Remove from the oven and keep the meat warm while you make the sauce.

Pour the marinade into the roasting pan and boil to reduce by two-thirds over a high heat, scraping up any bits stuck to the bottom of the pan. If you want a more elaborate sauce you can add herbs, brandy or port, cream or butter etc., but I like this simple gravy.

Serve the piece of beef on a long platter and take it to the table to carve.

INGREDIENTS

1½ lb piece of beef tenderloin
1 cup good red wine
2 tbsp olive oil
1 onion, sliced
1 carrot, chopped
1 celery stalk, chopped
2 garlic cloves, crushed
salt and freshly ground pepper

Serves 2 (plus leftovers)

Opposite: Sicilian Orange Sorbet
Below: Roast Beef Tenderloin

ROAST DUCK

INGREDIENTS

3 lb duck

2–3 garlic cloves (optional)

2 tbsp soy sauce

2 tbsp olive oil

2 tbsp good dessert wine

1 small fennel bulb, thinly sliced

2 carrots, thinly sliced

1 celery stalk, thinly sliced

1 small onion, thinly sliced

1 in fresh ginger root, peeled and thinly sliced

⅔ cup Vegetable or Light Meat Stock or good white wine

salt and freshly ground pepper (optional)

Serves 2

Preheat the oven to 400°.

Cut the wing pinions from the duck. If you are using garlic, insert slivers of it into the skin. Mix the soy sauce, oil and wine, and brush some of it over the duck.

Peel and slice the vegetables thinly, including the ginger root, and place in the bottom of a roasting pan. Prick the duck all over, particularly in the fatty parts, and place on the vegetables breast down. Put to roast in the oven for about 1½ hours.

After the first 30 minutes remove from the oven and carefully drain off the fat. Brush on a little more of the soy sauce mixture and pour a couple of spoonfuls of stock onto the vegetables. Do this again 30 minutes later.

When cooked, keep the duck warm while you finish the sauce. Drain off the rest of the fat. Pour the remaining stock or wine into the roasting pan and place on top of the stove. Bring to a boil, scraping up any bits stuck to the bottom of the pan. Add a little water, if necessary, and adjust the seasoning. Strain into a sauce boat and serve with the duck.

POT ROAST PARTRIDGES

INGREDIENTS

4 tbsp unsalted butter

1 tbsp finely chopped fresh herbs

salt and freshly ground pepper

2 partridges

1 tbsp brandy

2 tbsp port, red vermouth or red wine

1 tbsp clear fruit or herb jelly (see pages 80 and 81)

TO SERVE

small rounds of toast

Serves 2

For a really special treat there is little to beat partridge – it has a marvelously delicate flavor that remains gamey at the same time. I have heard the ideal breakfast, or lunch, described as "a cold partridge and half a bottle of Champagne." If your budget and your cooking pot will stretch to it, this is a very easy way of feeding a number of people – simply multiply the quantities by the number you are cooking for. At a pinch, one partridge could feed two.

Preheat the oven to 375°.

Mix 3 tablespoons of the butter with the herbs and seasoning. Smear some of the seasoned butter over the partridge breasts and put the rest inside the cavities.

Heat the remaining butter in a flameproof casserole and fry the birds all over until nicely browned. Pour on the brandy and set alight. Add the port.

Cover with a lid or foil and cook in the oven for 35 minutes or so. Test by sticking a skewer into the thigh; the juices will be clear if it is ready.

Drain the cooking juices into a small saucepan, add the fruit jelly, cook and reduce until you have about 3 tablespoons of sauce. Serve the partridge on small rounds of toast with a little sauce from the pan.

RICE STUFFING

The dense chestnut and sausage stuffing that is so often a part of the traditional British Christmas dinner is not very much to my taste, nor is the sage and onion with fine bread crumbs. I like something with a little more texture and crunch, and rice makes an admirable substitute.

One of the nicest stuffings I have ever tasted was simply a couple of handfuls of cooked wild rice flavored with herbs to which some chopped hazelnuts had been added. This was stuffed into a chicken that was then roasted. The stuffing recipe I give for the spring chicken on page 32 could just as easily be used here with the Roast Duck, or with the Pot Roast Partridges (see page 100). This recipe for rice stuffing would also be good for the spring chicken or the partridge or, indeed, for any dish which calls for a stuffing. It is a mixture that you can vary to suit your own tastes. Try this rice stuffing with chopped dried apricots and walnuts instead of raisins and pine nuts. Adjust the quantities given here for birds larger or smaller than 3 lb.

Chop the giblets very small and fry them in 1 tablespoon of butter. Allow them to cool, then mix them with the rest of the ingredients. Spoon the mixture into the body cavity and close it with skewers or toothpicks.

INGREDIENTS

liver, gizzard and heart of the bird
4 tbsp melted butter
2½ cups cooked rice, if possible a mixture of brown, wild and basmati
2 celery stalks, finely chopped
1 onion, finely chopped
2 garlic cloves, crushed
1 apple, grated
2 tbsp golden raisins
2 tbsp pine nuts or chopped almonds
6 cloves
1 heaping tbsp chopped thyme or oregano
salt and freshly ground pepper

Makes enough stuffing for a 3 lb duck

BAKED JERUSALEM ARTICHOKES

A dish of baked Jerusalem artichokes would go very well with any of the Christmas main courses I have suggested.

Preheat the oven to 350°.

Scrub the vegetables well and cut off any bruised or knobbly bits. Cut them into ¼ inch slices and drop into a large pan of boiling water. Simmer for 2 to 3 minutes and then drain.

Butter an ovenproof dish and put in a layer of artichokes. Season lightly then pour on a little sauce or cream. Dot with a little butter and sprinkle on half the cheese. Add the rest of the artichoke slices, more seasoning, sauce or cream, butter and grated cheese.

Bake in the oven (you can place them at the bottom of a hotter oven depending on what else you are cooking).

INGREDIENTS

1 lb Jerusalem artichokes
salt and freshly ground white pepper
⅔ cup thin béchamel sauce or light cream
1 tbsp unsalted butter
1 tbsp freshly grated Parmesan or Gruyère cheese (optional)

Serves 2

CHICKEN OR TURKEY FILO PASTRY PIE

INGREDIENTS

12 sheets filo pastry, about ½ lb

6 tbsp unsalted butter, melted

½ lb mushrooms, quickly fried

½ lb potatoes, cooked and diced

3 large eggs

5 tbsp strong Chicken Stock

5 tbsp light cream

2 tsp lemon juice

grated nutmeg

1 tbsp chopped fresh chives

salt and freshly ground pepper

4 cups cooked chicken or turkey meat cut into small cubes

3 ripe tomatoes, peeled, seeded and diced

4 scallions, chopped

2 sprigs of fresh French tarragon or basil

Serves 6

The remaining filo pastry from making the Oysters in Spinach Overcoats (page 97) can be put to good use in this large pie – it makes a suitable dish for a New Year's Eve party.

Preheat the oven to 325°.

Lay the sheets of pastry on a damp dish towel. Brush the top sheet with melted butter – it is easier to butter the pastry while it is still on the pile rather than fitted into the dish. Brush a shallow, rectangular dish, about 8 × 10 × 2 inches, with melted butter. Lay two sheets of buttered filo pastry in the dish, gently lining the dish with them; some pastry will overlap the edges of the dish. Lay two further sheets of buttered pastry on top and cut to fit the bottom of the dish.

Put the mushrooms and potatoes in the dish, fairly well packed together. Beat the eggs, stock and cream together with the lemon juice and nutmeg and pour a third of it over the mushroom and potato mixture. Sprinkle on the chives and season with salt and pepper.

Lay four more sheets of buttered filo pastry on top, cut to fit. Mix the chicken with the tomatoes and scallions and spread this on top of the pastry. Pour the rest of the egg mixture over the chicken. Chop up the fresh herbs and sprinkle these on top, together with a little more salt and pepper. Cut two more sheets of buttered pastry to fit the dish and lay these over the chicken. Fold the overlapping pastry over the top to make a neat parcel shape and finally lay two more buttered sheets on top, cut to fit the top exactly. With a sharp knife, lightly score the top layer into a diamond pattern.

Bake for 40 minutes, then increase the temperature to 400° and continue baking for 5 to 10 minutes to allow the pie to cook to a golden brown.

BROILED RADICCHIO AND GOAT CHEESE

INGREDIENTS

1 firm head round radicchio

2–3 tbsp good olive oil

salt and freshly ground pepper

4 slices of goat cheese

Serves 2

Radicchio is a surprisingly good vegetable to cook and not at all restricted to salads. Here it makes an excellent accompaniment to the cheese course.

Remove any bruised or wilted leaves and the root from the radicchio. Wash the radicchio and cut into 4 slices. Brush each slice with olive oil, lightly season and place under a preheated broiler, turning occasionally to cook it through.

Lay a slice of goat's cheese on each slice of radicchio and return it to the heat. Serve when the cheese is bubbling and browning. Even if a crust forms, it is delicious.

CHILLED PERSIMMON CREAMS

INGREDIENTS

2 ripe persimmons with sound,
unblemished skins

grated zest and juice of 1 small
lemon

1 scant tbsp confectioners' sugar

⅔ cup heavy cream

Serves 2

Just occasionally, at the end of the year, we are lucky enough to find the true persimmons imported from Italy. Full and swollen, they look far too ripe to eat, but this is when they have reached perfection. Sharon or kaki fruit can also be used for this recipe.

Take a thin slice off the top of each persimmon to make the lid. With a pointed spoon, carefully scoop out the flesh from one half persimmon, roughly chop this and reserve. Scoop out the rest of the persimmon flesh, keeping the skins intact, and put the flesh into a blender together with the lemon zest and juice and sugar. Blend until smooth.
  Whip the cream until firm. Fold in the persimmon purée and then the chopped persimmon. Divide the mixture among the two fruit skins, replace the lids and chill until required.

MINCEMEAT SOUFFLÉ

INGREDIENTS

2 tbsp unsalted butter

3 tbsp flour

⅔ cup scalded milk

4 tsp sugar

2 tbsp mincemeat

2 large eggs

Serves 2

Preheat the oven to 400°.
  Melt the butter in a heavy-based saucepan and stir in the flour. Cook over a low heat for 2 to 3 minutes, stirring continuously. Gradually add the hot milk to the mixture. This will thicken initially and seem lumpy, but just beat vigorously and allow the mixture to boil each time you add more milk. When all the milk has been added, stir the mixture until smooth and let it cook gently for 5 minutes.
  Butter two small ramekins and lightly sprinkle with sugar. Stir the remaining sugar and mincemeat into the white sauce. Separate the eggs and beat the egg yolks, one at a time, into the white sauce. Whisk the egg whites in a large bowl until stiff and fold them carefully into the soufflé mixture, using a metal spoon or plastic spatula, not a wooden spoon.
  Pour the mixture into the prepared ramekins and stand them in a roasting pan containing a little water. Bake in the oven for 10 to 12 minutes.

*Previous page: Broiled Radicchio
and Goat Cheese
Opposite: Chilled Persimmon
Creams*

DAY

Like all the other meals in this book this one really did take place, but not on a "moving day." It started as a project in which a couple of chefs and a couple of cooks were each asked to produce a good meal for four outdoors on nothing more than a two-burner camping gas stove with grill. We all discovered that it was indeed possible to produce delicious food despite difficult circumstances. Those circumstances might well include the day you move house, when you do not remember where you have packed your best pots, pans and knives, when your own stove has not yet been connected and you have only a camping stove. The meal I cooked worked extraordinarily well and required little in the way of equipment – I even strained the tagliatelle through a tennis racquet with success when we realized that we had not brought a colander with us!

Tom and I were not in quite such dire straits when we moved house but I do remember feeling it was important for us to take time out from decorating to sit down and enjoy a proper meal together. On that occasion we ate artichokes vinaigrette, osso bucco, spinach salad with bacon, cheese, and fresh mango, all washed down with a bottle of chilled 1976 Brauneberger Mandelgraben Spätlese.

In the menu here, Vegetable Fondue makes a nice variation on the ubiquitous crudités and dip, and I must say that the oil has a delicious flavor when cooled, strained and used on potato salad or in other dressings. An alternative would be to thread blanched vegetables on skewers and dip them into a garlicky dressing or mayonnaise. You can, of course, vary the vegetables to suit the season.

I wonder if you have tried red wine with fish? Both cooking it with a red wine sauce, and drinking red wine with it? It does work, I assure you. I have even used this red wine recipe with cod, not just the richer, oilier salmon and sea trout, and it worked well. The secret is to use a

Vegetable Fondue

Salmon Fillets in Red Wine Sauce
or
Shrimp with Garlic
or
Chicken with Walnuts

Tomatoes and Cheese on Toast

Hot Fruit Salad
or
Zabaglione

young fruity wine or, alternatively, a much older one from which the tannin has almost gone. I like to use a young wine, preferably one which has plenty of Cabernet Sauvignon or Cabernet franc which seems to keep the sauce a good red color rather than turning it brown. If you remain unconvinced about red wine with fish, you can replace it with white and add a little flavoring such as fennel or French tarragon.

If you want to cook this recipe in the winter then you will have to use farmed salmon. The wild is only available in season, from February/March to the first week of September. The farmed variety is not as good in my view because it does not have the same firm texture. How can it when it has been kept swimming around in sheltered conditions rather than in the wild? It is also fed rather than having to hunt for its own food.

The recipe for Salmon Fillets in Red Wine Sauce can be presented with tagliatelle; the two alternatives that follow – Shrimp with Garlic, and Chicken with Walnuts – are even more simple, and can be stir-fried in a single pan.

If your moving day is so fraught that you could not contemplate cooking a meal, at least break for a snack. Tomatoes and Cheese on Toast is one of the all-time greats, especially when you can find perfectly ripe, sweet tomatoes and pair them with a not-too-young goat cheese and toast the whole thing to a bubbling golden brown. Such a dish would indeed be worthy of a place as an appetizer, cheese course or savory at a grand dinner party. The Hot Fruit Salad, too, although it is simplicity itself to cook, has such a rich texture and complex flavor that it would satisfy the most critical guest, let alone a couple of hungry furniture-movers. An equally satisfying and simple dessert that requires even fewer ingredients is the Zabaglione, which can be prepared in only minutes at the end of the meal.

The last time I cooked Salmon Fillets in Red Wine Sauce we drank with it one of the excellent value Cabernet Sauvignons from Australia, which I also used in the cooking; a Californian equivalent from the same grape variety would work equally well.

TIMING
The dishes all require last-minute cooking, so it is best to make one dish at a time and eat it before cooking the next.

VEGETABLE FONDUE

It is quite important to choose vegetables that will take roughly the same amount of time to cook. There will be plenty of oil left over, which can be used to brush fish, vegetables or meat for grilling or broiling.

Wash, dry and prepare the vegetables. Broccoli should be broken into florets, cherry tomatoes should be left whole, button or cap mushrooms cut into quarters, zucchini sliced on the diagonal, snow peas topped and tailed. Thread the vegetables onto 8 wooden skewers.

Put the oil, anchovies with their oil, garlic, olives and herb in a blender or food processor and process until smooth. Pour into a small, heavy saucepan and bring slowly to a boil.

When the flavored oil is hot, pour it into a fondue pot and place over a Sterno burner on the table. Cook the vegetables in the flavored oil, at table.

INGREDIENTS

½ lb mixed vegetables, at least 3 varieties
2 cups olive oil
1 small can of anchovies
2 plump garlic cloves, chopped
4 olives, black or green, pitted
sprig of fresh rosemary, sage, thyme or marjoram

Serves 2

Vegetable Fondue

SALMON FILLETS IN RED WINE SAUCE

INGREDIENTS

¾ lb salmon fillets, skinned

2 tbsp unsalted butter

1 tbsp chopped shallots

½ cup Cabernet Sauvignon

Serves 2

Sea trout can be used in this recipe instead, as can white wine.

Trim the fillets into neat shapes. Melt half the butter in a heavy frying pan and lay the fillets in it, skin side up (although the skin has, of course, been removed). Add the shallots. Cook gently for 2 minutes, then carefully turn the fish over and cook for 1 or 2 minutes longer, depending on the thickness. Remove the fish to a plate and keep it warm (over the pan in which you cook the tagliatelle, for example).

Raise the heat under the pan, pour in the wine and let it bubble fiercely to boil off the alcohol, scraping up any bits stuck to the bottom of the pan. When the wine has reduced by half and become syrupy add the rest of the butter, swirling it to emulsify it with the sauce.

Serve the fish on heated dinner plates, with some sauce and freshly cooked tagliatelle.

Salmon Fillets in Red Wine Sauce

SHRIMP WITH GARLIC

On those days when you do not have all your kitchen equipment at hand it makes little sense to use recipes that require a good deal of measuring. For this one you need only a large frying pan or wok, a wooden spoon and a tablespoon for measuring.

This is a most versatile recipe and it does wonders for frozen shrimp. As it stands it is redolent of *tapas* bars in Seville, or the shellfish restaurants in Lisbon. Change the olive oil to sesame and peanut oils, add some finely shredded fresh ginger, a splash of soy sauce and some rice wine and the dish might remind you of a meal eaten in a little restaurant in Kowloon, or something you smelled cooking on a street hawker's stall in Singapore.

If the shrimp are frozen, allow them to thaw before cooking them. Heat the oil in a frying pan and add the shrimp, garlic and scallions. Cook for about 5 minutes, turning the shrimp over at least once. Sprinkle on the parsley, salt if needed, and pepper.

If you are using whisky or brandy, pour it on and light it at arm's length. When the flames have died down, the shrimp are ready for eating. It is a messy dish, best eaten in the fingers with plenty of bread to soak up the delicious cooking juices.

INGREDIENTS

1 lb medium shrimp in their shells

2–3 tbsp olive oil

2–3 garlic cloves, finely chopped

2 scallions, finely chopped

1 tbsp chopped parsley

salt (optional)

freshly ground pepper

1 tbsp whisky or brandy (optional)

Serves 2

CHICKEN WITH WALNUTS

INGREDIENTS

9 oz chicken breast

1 tsp sesame oil

1 tbsp soy sauce

pinch of five-spice powder

freshly ground pepper

1 tbsp peanut oil

1 celery stalk, sliced

1 carrot, sliced

3 scallions, sliced

2 oz snow peas, topped and tailed

14 walnut halves

1 tbsp walnut oil or peanut oil

2 tbsp rice wine or dry sherry

2 tbsp Chicken Stock or water

freshly ground pepper

salt (optional)

Serves 2

A good accompaniment is a bowl of fluffy steamed rice.

Remove the skin from the meat and cut it into small diagonal slivers about 1½ × ½ inch. Mix the sesame oil, soy sauce, five-spice powder and pepper in a bowl and stir in the chicken pieces. Cover and refrigerate for an hour or two, or overnight.

To cook, heat the peanut oil in a frying pan or wok and then add the vegetables in the order listed, giving the celery and carrot the longest cooking time (but no more than about 5 to 6 minutes) before you add the chicken pieces.

Stir-fry the chicken and vegetables for about 5 minutes, then add the walnuts, walnut oil, rice wine and stock. Cook for another couple of minutes on a high heat to reduce the liquid slightly. Add pepper to taste, and salt if you think the dish needs it – it probably will not since you have used soy sauce at an earlier stage.

Opposite: Tomatoes and Cheese on Toast

TOMATOES AND CHEESE ON TOAST

Whether cooked as a snack, an hors d'oeuvre or a cheese course, this simple dish is always delicious. It is one of our favorite standbys.

Brush the bread with olive oil on both sides. Toast under the broiler on one side. Lay the tomato slices on the untoasted side, season with salt and pepper and place a round of goat cheese on top. Replace under the hot broiler and cook until the cheese is golden and bubbling.

INGREDIENTS

4 slices cut from a French loaf, or 4 circles cut from sliced bread with a pastry cutter

1 tbsp extra virgin olive oil

4 slices of tomato

salt and freshly ground pepper

4 slices cut from a cylindrical goat cheese

Serves 2

HOT FRUIT SALAD

INGREDIENTS

½ lb firm fruit

1 small ripe banana

2 tbsp fresh orange or lemon juice

a little sugar, if required

2 tbsp liqueur or spirit

Serves 2

Any firm fruit can be used to make a successful salad: apples, pears, plums or apricots. A mixture of fruit can be used, but I think it is nicer to stick to one, and to use a matching liqueur or spirit such as a Calvados, pear eau-de-vie, slivovitz, etc. Very cold *crème fraîche* or thick plain Greek yogurt is an excellent accompaniment.

Prepare the fruit. Apples and pears do not need peeling but should be quartered and cored. Pits should be removed from other fruit. Slice the fruit, together with the banana, into a nonstick frying pan. Cook in the fruit juice until the main fruit is just tender but not mushy. By this time the banana will have cooked down to a delicious sauce. Add sugar if you think it is needed.

Raise the heat, pour on the spirit, stand back and light it at arm's length. Serve immediately the flames have died down.

ZABAGLIONE

INGREDIENTS

2 tbsp marsala (or sherry or port)

2 egg yolks

TO SERVE

ladyfingers, langues de chat or
  almond macaroons

Serves 2

This is a very easy dessert to make *à la minute,* and one that requires little in the way of ingredients.

Place a dessert basin or other heatproof mixing bowl over a pot of hot water (the water should not touch the bottom of the basin) and put the pot on low heat to maintain the water temperature. It is important to keep the water *below* boiling, otherwise the egg yolk will start to cook rather than just thicken and you will end up with something like scrambled egg on the bottom of the basin.

Put the wine into the basin and let it warm up. Add the egg yolks and start whisking. Gradually, after some minutes, the mixture will begin to turn frothy and become paler and paler. After more whisking it will become denser and richer and will probably begin to brim over the top of the basin. Scoop into wine glasses and serve warm with ladyfingers, langues de chat or almond macaroons.

If you wish to serve the dessert cold, remove the basin from the pot once the froth has reached its full volume. Continue whisking, away from the heat, until the mixture is quite cold. Spoon into wine glasses and keep in the refrigerator until needed.

Opposite: Hot Fruit Salad

PLANNED

Economy

This is an elegant meal that initially sounds extravagant but is not in fact so. It really is worth buying a whole duckling, or indeed any bird, just for two because there is much you can do with the rest of it. Having used the duck breasts as the main course you can use the leftover legs and thighs to make rillettes, a cassoulet, a duck and olive casserole, or stuffing for ravioli. Then, of course, there is the carcass, from which you will make excellent soup. Some of these recipes produce enough leftovers for four, and sometimes six, people. Take the opportunity to invite your friends to join you for dinner!

Again I have cooked in red wine and again it is a wine with plenty of Cabernet, this time the Cabernet franc that does so well in the Loire valley. Chinon, like its close neighbor Bourgueil across the river, is one of our favorite wines and one that Tom and I are always pleased to see on wine lists outside France. It is a lovely crisp wine with lots of fruit which makes it an ideal partner for duck.

Look for other complementary flavors and textures by serving plenty of crisp leaves in your salad and crisp vegetables with it. If you do not like cabbages in any form then fennel, even when cooked, retains an agreeable crunch like celery and goes very well with the duck.

When serving a rich meat it is, I feel, a good idea to provide cold, refreshing dishes before and after it, and a salad and a sorbet are the ideal choices. A warm salad, the kind of dish described on restaurant menus as *salade tiède*, *salade folle* and *salade fantaisie*, makes a perfect appetizer, being as versatile as your imagination. There is a danger, however. In restaurants I have come across such a dish where the chef has piled langoustines on top of foie gras, and garnished them with truffles and caviar. It is not a question of piling ingredients, and expensive ingredients, on top of each other. What you are aiming to do is to whet the appetite, not satisfy it in the first few mouthfuls. Small amounts of any of the above ingredients served with good crisp

DUCK BREASTS IN CHINON WITH STIR-FRIED MIXED CABBAGE

Duck Liver and Roquefort Salad

Duck Breasts in Chinon
or
Duck and Green Olive Casserole
Stir-Fried Mixed Cabbage

Mango Sorbet with Jasmine Tea Sauce
or
Mango Mousse

---

leaves and your favorite dressing leave the impression of rich, rare food at limited cost. You could make further use of the duck here to create the marvelous combination of duck livers with Roquefort.

The same strictures apply to the sorbet. Do not try to impress with three or four sorbets and their accompanying sauces and a few slices of fruit to match. Again, two flavors are more appealing. The mangoes can equally well be transformed into a light mousse. Use cottage cheese to replace the more usual cream for a subtle, new flavor.

TIMING

Apart from the sorbet and its sauce, which should be prepared in advance, the rest of the dishes are best cooked *à la minute,* when required. Salad leaves and vegetables can be washed, trimmed and prepared as appropriate before you start the final cooking.

DUCK LIVER AND ROQUEFORT SALAD

Prepare the salad at the last minute for maximum freshness. It is particularly good to eat while the duck liver is still warm.

Clean and trim the liver, carefully removing any greenish parts and the sinews. Soaking the liver in milk for a few hours in advance will improve the color and flavor. Dry the liver in paper towels and slice into several pieces.

Mix together the oil, lemon juice, salt and pepper in the proportions you prefer for your salad dressings. Toss your salad greens in the dressing and add the cheese. Arrange on individual plates.

Heat a heavy frying pan. Put a few drops of oil in the frying pan, enough to stop the livers from sticking, and when smoking put in the liver. Fry for 2 to 3 minutes, shaking the pan a few times but not stirring as this tends to break up the livers. When ready, that is, still slightly pink in the middle when you stick a knife point in, place the liver pieces on top of the salad. Pour on any pan juices and serve while still warm.

INGREDIENTS

2 oz duck or chicken liver

a little milk (optional)

extra virgin olive oil

lemon juice

salt and freshly ground pepper

2 oz (1-2 cups) of any or all of the following salad greens: lettuce, chicory, Belgian endive, arugula, watercress or other salad leaves

2 oz Roquefort cheese, cut into cubes

Serves 2

Duck Liver and Roquefort Salad

HOMEMADE RAVIOLI
STUFFED WITH DUCK

INGREDIENTS

FOR THE PASTA

2 large eggs

1 cup bread flour

⅓ cup fine semolina flour

FOR THE FILLING

½ cup chopped cooked lean duck meat

¼ cup ricotta cheese

½ cup chopped cooked mushrooms

1 garlic clove

salt and freshly ground pepper

plenty of freshly grated nutmeg

TO SERVE

extra virgin olive oil or unsalted butter

fresh sage or rosemary leaves

freshly grated parmesan cheese

Serves 2 (as a main course)

In a food processor, work the three pasta ingredients until crumbly and beginning to stick together, then knead into a ball with your hands. Break off an egg-sized piece and start to knead, flatten and roll it through a pasta machine. Keep putting the piece of pasta through the machine until it is as thin and transparent as you can get it without tearing it. Repeat with the remaining pasta. If you do not have a pasta machine, roll out the dough, taking an egg-sized piece at a time, until it is about 1/16 inch thick.

Mix together all the ingredients for the filling until they are thoroughly blended, or process them until smooth in a food processor.

Cut out circles of pasta 2–3 inches in diameter with a pastry cutter. Put a little filling on each. Moisten the edges, fold in half and pinch the edges together. Allow to dry spread out on a dish towel.

To cook, drop the ravioli into plenty of boiling water, boil vigorously and drain when *al dente*. This can take 30 seconds to 5 minutes or more, depending on how dry the pasta is when you cook it. Remove the ravioli with a slotted spoon and place in a lightly oiled or buttered dish. Serve with more oil or melted butter in which you've infused fresh sage or rosemary leaves, and some freshly grated parmesan.

DUCK RILLETTES

If you have used duck breasts to make Duck Breasts in Chinon in this menu, turn the uncooked leftovers into rillettes. The recipe can also be used for pork alone, using double the quantity of pork sides, or rabbit (in which case you will need twice as much pork as rabbit), or goose and pork sides in equal quantities.

Preheat the oven to 300–350°.

Put the pork, duck legs, duck skin and fat in a casserole. Add the seasoning and water. Cook at the bottom of the oven for 3 to 4 hours or until all the fat has melted and the meat is cooked.

Place a sieve over a bowl. Discard the bones and any skin from the casserole and ladle some of the remaining meat and fat into the sieve. Take a fork in each hand and literally pull the meat apart. It should all finish up in shreds. Pack loosely into a jar, crock or pâté dish and add a little of the melted fat. Continue until all the meat has been shredded and potted and all the fat poured around it. Make sure that the top has a good layer of fat, which will form the seal once refrigerated.

NOTE ON POTTED MEATS AND FISH

Rillettes are not very far removed from the English potted meat, which is essentially cooked meat, pounded to a paste and mixed with a little fat to make it unctuous and spreadable. When homemade it is a far cry from the nasty little jars of sticky, smelly paste that are sold in many English food stores.

With a food processor you can make all manner of potted meat and fish. All you need to do is cut the cooked meat into pieces and put it in the bowl of the food processor with the same quantity of softened butter, perhaps a little wine, some seasoning and herbs, and process until smooth.

Try venison with port and nutmeg, salmon with vermouth and chives, chicken with sherry and mace, duck with orange liqueur and black pepper. It is a very good way of using up cooked leftovers.

INGREDIENTS

½ lb fresh pork sides, sliced
duck legs, chopped
duck skin with plenty of fat on it, plus any more fat from the cavity
salt and freshly ground pepper
1 bay leaf
dried sage
grated nutmeg
1¼ cups water

Serves 6 to 8

DUCK BREASTS IN CHINON

INGREDIENTS

2 half duck breasts, skinned

2/3 cup Chinon

1 celery stalk, diced

1 small onion, diced

1 medium carrot, diced

2 garlic cloves, crushed

5 tbsp duck stock

1 tsp mixed peppercorns

2 tbsp unsalted butter

1 tsp sunflower oil

Serves 2

Wild duck, guinea fowl, chicken or wild goose can be used in this recipe. For the last two, cooking times will need to be a little longer.

Marinate the meat for several hours in the wine together with the vegetables and garlic. Remove the meat from the marinade and dry it thoroughly. Put the marinade in a saucepan together with the stock and simmer for 10 minutes: the vegetables will impart their flavor and the alcohol will evaporate from the wine, leaving just its rich flavor and color behind. Put the peppercorns into a cup and strain the liquid over them.

Heat half the butter and the oil in a heavy frying pan. Add the duck breasts. Cook on a high heat for 3 minutes, then turn over carefully and cook for a further 2 to 3 minutes. Remove from the pan and keep on a warm plate while you make the sauce. Add the liquid and peppercorns to the frying pan and boil to reduce by half or until syrupy. Add the rest of the butter, a little at a time, over an even heat and shake the pan to emulsify the butter with the sauce.

Spoon the sauce onto heated dinner plates and place the duck breasts on top, simply carved into oblique slices.

Duck Breasts in Chinon with Stir-Fried Mixed Cabbage

DUCK AND GREEN OLIVE CASSEROLE

The casserole goes well with rice, and any leftover meat and gravy make a good sauce for pasta.

Remove the fat and skin from the duck. Fry a small piece of skin in a heavy flameproof casserole until the fat runs; discard the skin. Add the onion and garlic and fry until golden brown. Remove and put to one side.

Fry the duck pieces until golden brown. Add the celery together with the onion and garlic mixture and the orange zest. Pit the olives if you wish (if not, remember to warn your guests) and add them to the casserole, together with the stock and wine. Tie the thyme and bay leaf together, stick the cloves into the bay leaf and tuck into the casserole. Season with salt and pepper.

Cover and simmer very gently, or cook in the oven preheated to 325–350°, for an hour or so or until the duck is tender.

INGREDIENTS

4 duck pieces
1 onion, thinly sliced
2 garlic cloves, thinly sliced
2 celery stalks, sliced
sliver (about 2–3 in) of thinly pared orange zest
2/3 cup green olives
2/3 cup duck stock
2/3 cup dry white wine
sprig of fresh thyme
1 bay leaf
3 cloves
salt and freshly ground pepper

Serves 2 to 4

CASSOULET

Start preparing the beans the day before required. Cover them with cold water, bring very slowly to a boil and boil them fast for 15 minutes. Drain, rinse and place in a large bowl. Cover well with boiling water and let them soak overnight, or for at least 6 hours; drain.

Preheat the oven to 300–350°.

Trim any excess fat off the meat, then lightly fry it in a non-stick pan to brown it all over. Remove and put to one side. Fry the onions, celery and garlic for a few minutes and place them in a deep casserole or other pot. Next put in a layer of soaked beans and season lightly. Add the lamb chops next, followed by more beans, the duck pieces, more beans and finally the sausage chunks. Add the tomatoes and bay leaves and pour on the stock. Cover the casserole and cook in the oven for 2 to 2½ hours.

Remove from the oven, uncover the pot and sprinkle the bread crumbs on top. Return to the oven and bake uncovered for a further 20 minutes. Serve straight from the pot.

INGREDIENTS

1 2/3 cups dried navy or cannellini beans
2 duck legs, each chopped at the joint
4 rib lamb chops
2 onions, sliced
1 celery stalk, sliced
4 garlic cloves, sliced
salt and freshly ground pepper
3/4 lb spicy sausage (salami, chorizo), cut into chunks
1/2 lb tomatoes, chopped
2 bay leaves
2½ cups duck, Chicken or other meat or Vegetable Stock
1½ cups fresh bread crumbs

Serves 4

STIR-FRIED MIXED CABBAGE

INGREDIENTS

1 tbsp peanut oil

2½-3 cups shredded cabbage (a mixture of Napa cabbage, bok choy, savoy cabbage, winter cabbage, etc.)

1 tbsp brown sugar

1 tbsp raspberry or black currant vinegar

½ tsp cumin seeds

Serves 2

Cooking cabbage this way seems to do away with that pervasive cabbagey smell that used to put me off even cooking it.

Heat the oil in a wok or frying pan and when smoking stir in the cabbage. When this is turning translucent, sprinkle on the sugar and stir-fry until melted. Moisten with the vinegar and add the cumin seeds. When the vinegar and sugar have begun to caramelize, the cabbage is ready. Serve hot.

If you are serving Duck Breasts in Chinon you can, if you wish, place the duck slices on top of a pile of shredded cabbage sitting in a pool of sauce.

MANGO MOUSSE

INGREDIENTS

1 envelope unflavored gelatin

1¼ cups clear apple juice

½ cup cottage cheese

1 ripe, fragrant mango

sugar to taste

2 egg whites

FOR THE GARNISH

toasted sliced almonds

Serves 2 to 4

Here is a recipe for using a mango that produces a deliciously light, clean-tasting dessert, and one that has no cream. If the mango is very ripe the dish should be sweet enough without adding any sugar.

Soften the gelatin in a little of the apple juice. Heat half of the apple juice, add the gelatin and stir until it has dissolved.

Sieve the cottage cheese and put it in the blender. Peel the mango over the blender to catch as much of the juice as possible, put in the fruit pulp, the gelatin mixture and the remaining juice. Blend until smooth. Add sugar if necessary.

Whisk the egg whites until stiff and fold into the mango mixture. Pour into a dish, chill and set. Garnish with toasted almonds.

MANGO SORBET WITH JASMINE TEA SAUCE

Consider transposing the recipe: a jasmine tea sorbet with a mango sauce.

Slice the mango in half down both sides of the pit and scoop out all the flesh from the skins into a measuring cup; remove as much flesh as possible from the pit. Add apple juice to make up to 1¼ cups. Pour into a blender and blend until smooth. Freeze, either in a sorbetière or automatic ice cream-maker, according to directions.

    Meanwhile, make the sauce. Put the tea leaves, and as many dried jasmine flowers as possible, into a pitcher and pour on the boiling water. Allow to steep for 10 minutes. Strain into a saucepan and stir in the sugar. When the sugar has melted, bring to a boil and continue boiling until syrupy and reduced to about 6 tablespoons. Remove from the heat and allow to go cold, then chill.

    Serve the sorbet with a little sauce.

INGREDIENTS

1 ripe mango
unsweetened apple juice
1 tbsp jasmine tea leaves
1¼ cups boiling water
2 tbsp sugar

Serves 2

Mango Sorbet with Jasmine Tea Sauce

ACKNOWLEDGEMENTS

AUTHOR'S ACKNOWLEDGEMENTS

I would like to thank Graham Miller and Maxine Clark for making this food look good enough to eat; Eleanor Lines for her sensitive and intelligent guardianship of the book in all its stages; Norma MacMillan for all the questions she asked and made me ask myself; Tricia Hilder for typing the manuscript and Tom Bissell for eating his way constructively through these ten dinner parties for two and more.

PICTURE CREDITS

The photographs in this book were taken by Graham Miller, assisted by Nicholas Rigg. The artwork illustrations are by Christopher White.

OTHER ACKNOWLEDGEMENTS

The editors would like to thank: Valerie Chandler, Fiona Duncan, Katherine Judge, Joan Lee, Wendy Lee, Antony Mason, Rob Mitchell, Sophia Ollard.

INDEX

R

Rabbit *70, 121*
Radicchio: Broiled radicchio and
goat cheese *94,* 102, **103**
Ravioli *28, 50*
Homemade ravioli stuffed with
duck 120
Red currants: Tomato and red
currant soup *38–40, 41,* 43
Rhubarb *81*
Chilled rhubarb soup *84,* 86, **87**
Rhubarb sauce 36
Rice *18*
Asparagus and white wine
risotto *18,* 22, **22**
Lemon rice pudding 74, 90, **91**
Rice stuffing 101
Rice, Wild *29,* 33, 101
Roast duck 92, 100, *101*
Roast beef tenderloin *92–4,* **93,**
95, 99, **99**
Rosé Champagne granita *26, 29,*
34, **35**
Rosemary flowers: Carrot and
rosemary flower soup *38, 41,*
42, **42**
Rosemary jelly 81

S

Salads 45, 46, *52,* 77, *116,* 119
Salad dressing *45*
Salmon *60,* 85, *121*
Salmon fillets in red wine sauce
106–8, 110, **110**
Smoked salmon shapes *95,* 96,
96
Scallops *28*
Mousseline of scallop roe *28,* 30,
31
Scallops with julienne of
vegetables *28,* 30
Shellfish *50, 52,* 92
Shrimp *16, 92*
Shrimp with garlic 111
Sicilian orange sorbet *94, 95,* 98,
98
Smoked salmon shapes *95,* 96, **96**
Snails baked in new potatoes 20
Sorbet 98, 125
Soufflé *84, 94–5,* 104
Soups *38–9, 42,* 43, 44, 63, 64,
74, 86
Spaghetti: Bean and vegetable
soup *70, 73,* 74, **75**
Spinach: Oysters in spinach
overcoats 92, *95, 97,* **97**

Squab (pigeon) *70*
Squab chicken: Stuffed squab
chicken with vegetables **27,**
28, 29, 32, **33**
Steak *see* Beef
Stir-fried green vegetables *60,* 68,
68
Stir-fried mixed cabbage **117,** 124
Stock *13,* 14, 15, *40*
Strawberries in Beaujolais *41*
Strawberries with honey and
balsamic vinegar *52, 53,* 58,
59
Stuffed squab chicken with
vegetables **27,** *28, 29, 32,* **33**
Stuffing 101

T

Tarragon
Broccoli, pear and tarragon
soup *38–40, 41,* 43
Tarragon pot-roasted quail *40,*
41, 46, **47**
Terrine: Oxtail terrine *82,* 86
Thimble dumplings 88, *89*
Tomatoes *8–9, 11, 40*
Gazpacho Andaluz *60,* 64
Ketchup *45*
Tomato and garlic soup *38–40,*
41, 44
Tomato and red currant soup
38–40, 41, 43
Tomato, basil and cardamom
salad *39, 45,* **45**
Tomatoes and cheese on toast
108, 113, **113**
Tuna fish *70*
Turbot with laver sauce **51,** *53,* 56
Turkey filo pastry pie *92,* 102

V

Vegetables *18, 26–8; see also*
Potatoes, *etc.*
Bean and vegetable soup *70,*
73, 74, **75**
Scallops with julienne of
vegetables *28,* 30
Stir-fried green vegetables *60,*
68, **68**
Vegetable fondue *106,* **107,** *108,*
109, **109**
Vegetable stock *13,* 14, *40*
Venison *70, 121*
Medallions of venison
marinated in pomegranate
70–2, 73, 76, **77**

Vinaigrette *45*
Vinegars *11–12, 52*

W

Walnuts: Hedgerow salad with
walnut and arugula dressing
16–18, 23
Warm potato salad *41,* 46, **47**
Wild rice *29,* 33, 101
Wines *18–19, 41, 52–3, 62, 72–3,*
84, 95, 106–8, 116; see also
Champagne

Y

Yogurt *13*
Rose hearts 36

Z

Zabaglione *108,* 114